Correlative Archaeology

ISSUES IN SOUTHWEST ARCHAEOLOGY

Edited by John Kantner

Mission Statement

Issues in Southwest Archaeology is dedicated to publishing volumes that critically evaluate current archaeological research in the US Southwest and Northwest Mexico. The books consider topics that are pervasive themes both in the archaeology of the region but also in contemporary anthropological inquiry, such as ethnicity, gender, migration, and violence. Written by leading scholars in the field, the volumes discuss more than just what archaeologists know about the prehistory of the Southwest; they also consider issues that impact the practice of archaeology today, including the roles of cultural resource management, oral history, and cultural property rights. Each contribution to the series is guided by the research interests and theoretical perspective of the author, but each book is ultimately synthetic, comparative, and fully engaged in broader anthropological interests.

Books in the Series

Correlative Archaeology: Rethinking Archaeological Theory, by
    Fumi Arakawa
*From Huhugam to Hohokam: Heritage and Archaeology in the American
    Southwest*, by J. Brett Hill
Agricultural Beginnings in the American Southwest, by Barbara J. Roth
The Archaeology of Art in the American Southwest, by Marit K. Munson
Living Histories: Native Americans and Southwestern Archaeology, by Chip
    Colwell-Chanthaphonh
*Art in the Pre-Hispanic Southwest: An Archaeology of Native American
    Cultures*, by Radosław Palonka

Correlative Archaeology

Rethinking Archaeological Theory

Fumi Arakawa

LEXINGTON BOOKS
Lanham • Boulder • New York • London

Published by Lexington Books
An imprint of The Rowman & Littlefield Publishing Group, Inc.
4501 Forbes Boulevard, Suite 200, Lanham, Maryland 20706
www.rowman.com

86-90 Paul Street, London EC2A 4NE

British Library Cataloguing in Publication Information Available

Library of Congress Cataloging-in-Publication Data

Names: Arakawa, Fumi, author.
  Title: Correlative archaeology : rethinking archaeological theory / Fumi
    Arakawa.
  Other titles: Rethinking archaeological theory
  Description: Lanham : Lexington Books, [2022] | Series: Issues in Southwest
    archaeology | Includes bibliographical references and index. | Summary:
    "Fumi Arakawa, a Japanese scholar who was trained in Western
    archaeology, uses correlative thinking practices, which are derived from
    an East Asian view of the world that stresses connectivity, to analyze
    American Southwest artifacts within the prehistoric landscape of their
    origin"-- Provided by publisher.
  Identifiers: LCCN 2022004070 (print) | LCCN 2022004071 (ebook) | ISBN
    9781793643780 (cloth) | ISBN 9781793643797 (epub)
  Subjects: LCSH: Mimbres culture. | Indians of North America--New
    Mexico--Mimbres River Valley--Antiquities. | Mimbres River Valley
    (N.M.)--Antiquities. | Archaeology--Methodology.
  Classification: LCC E99.M76 A735 2022 (print) | LCC E99.M76 (ebook) | DDC
    978.9/01--dc23/eng/20220131
  LC record available at https://lccn.loc.gov/2022004070
  LC ebook record available at https://lccn.loc.gov/2022004071

To my friend and mentor, Spencer Nutima, who passed away in 2019, for his generous support, and to my parents, Takeshi and Michiko Arakawa, for their encouragement and tolerance

Contents

List of Figures

List of Tables

Preface

This book is about the interpretation of ancient artifacts and landscape. More particularly it is about the interpretation of Native American artifacts and its surrounding landscape by a Japanese person who was trained in Western archaeology. One might say that it is the convergence of three worlds— Western, Native American, and Eastern. One might also wonder how being Japanese affects the act of interpretation. This book is about correlating my mind, the artifacts, and my vocational training. In this capacity, I hope that you will find it interesting as an exercise of reflecting on the art of interpretation. It is also about correlating different methods of interpretations in ways that extend beyond a particular body. In this capacity, I hope that it is useful to you.

EAST MEETS WEST IN NATIVE AMERICA: LOCATING THE INTERPRETER

I grew up in Komaki city (a suburb of Nagoya city), located in central Japan. It is a landscape characterized by many rice fields, small rivers, and mountains. On Komaki Mountain, which rises above the city, there is a castle that dates back to the AD 1500s. I lived in Komaki until I was nineteen years old, and like many people at that age, I had no idea what I wanted to do. I was a part-time truck driver thinking about becoming a full-time truck driver, and my interests were to spend time with my friends, find a partner, and save money to travel abroad.

In particular, I wanted to go to America, or as we called it アメリカ (it is pronounced the same but without the r-sound [A-me-r/li-ca]). I had a Japanese aunt who lived with her American husband in Idaho, and when I had enough money saved, I asked if I could come for a visit. I wanted to see the landscape I experienced in John Wayne and Clint Eastwood movies (also

Young Guns) with my own eyes. I guess you could say I was captivated by the cowboy and Indian mythology of the American West.

Although I only had a short adventure in mind, my aunt and uncle thought I came to study English, which meant they expected me to stay—and stay and study I did. I enrolled in an English as a Second Language (ESL) program at a community college and eventually became a professor of archaeology at a university in the American Southwest. Of course, along the way, there were several formative experiences that have shaped my thinking and the ways in which I interpret artifacts and landscape.

After finishing my ESL program and Associate Degree in Art and Science, I transferred to the University of Idaho (U of I) with the intention of studying philosophy. Coming to the United States and finding myself in a predominantly white community, I became acutely aware of my cultural difference. Not only did I look different, but I realized that I thought much differently than those around me. This recognition of difference had two effects: I wanted to learn more about the people around me, and I wanted to better understand the philosophy that shaped me. In hindsight, it was an irony that I was not interested in East Asian philosophies, such as Taoism, Confucianism, and Buddhism, until I came to the United States, and in a certain light, you might say that this was the beginning of my journey in anthropology and later archaeology.

In order to learn more about Eastern and Western perspectives, I continued to study cultural anthropology at the U of I for my master's degree. One summer, I had an opportunity to participate in an archaeological project as an intern at the Nez Perce Reservation in Idaho that was led by an archaeology professor and sponsored by the Department of Fish and Wildlife. Although the project was conducted on Native land within a Native community, I noticed there were no Native American participants involved in the study, which I found odd. We were excavating a 4,000-year-old village, and one would assume that they might know something of interest to us, if not be interested in the village themselves. In hindsight, one might also say that I was naïve about the colonial past and present of American archaeology.

I enjoyed the research and loved being outside in the landscape, but what resonated most with me from that experience was my encounters with the Native American culture. One memory that stood out was when I was invited to participate in a pipe ceremony with Nez Perce elders, which I enjoyed (even though I was trying to quit smoking). The interactions with the Nez Perce community made me wonder: *Why don't Native Americans investigate the archaeological remains of their own ancestors? And, why instead do Euro-American archaeologists carry out this archaeological research and receive their status and salary?*

In some ways, this question was derived from my inability to understand the colonial legacy between anthropologists and Native Americans. However, in other ways, I wonder if it also reflects my experience of not being curious about my culture until I came to the United States. If, for example, one grows up with a castle overlooking their city, it doesn't seem as extraordinary or curious as it might to an outsider who has never seen a castle.

Fortunately, I had the opportunity to participate in an internship at the Crow Canyon Archaeological Center (CCAC) in Colorado. The Communities Through Time project, which focused on temporal changes of large ancestral Pueblo villages in the central Mesa Verde region through time, was designed to promote collaboration between archaeologists and Native Americans. The internship was a formative experience that not only showed me that collaborations between Western archaeologists and Native Americans were possible, but also taught me that Native Americans did have a great deal of interest in their culture and brought interpretations that were not accessible to academic approaches.

When I decided to pursue a PhD in archaeology at Washington State University (WSU) in Pullman, however, I learned why collaborations were not widely practiced. Trained as a processual archaeologist, it became apparent that reliance on scientific instruments was not conducive to incorporating Native perspectives. When I began studying archaeology at WSU, the majority of faculty members followed the processual archaeology paradigm (i.e., the emphasis on scientific studies or positive perspectives) and thus I was trained in positivist (or scientific) methods and theories of archaeology that did not value or create room for Native perspectives. For my dissertation research, I conducted a cost-benefit analysis, derived from an economic model, of tool-stone procurement patterns in order to understand and reconstruct how Ancestral Pueblo people procured or traded their raw materials— something of interest to academic archaeologists, but something that also methodologically and institutionally excluded Native perspectives.

On the basis of these experiences—my fascination with the East Asian philosophy that shaped me, my wondering about why Native peoples were not involved in researching their own history, and my scientific training which systematically excluded Native perspectives—I was induced to reflect and reexamine how I interpret artifacts and landscape. This awareness is especially important in my current position as the museum director at New Mexico State University (NMSU), where I am in charge of an archaeological collection that includes a number of Native American artifacts. As I became more aware of Native American issues, I made more of an effort to include them in the work I was doing. However, the question of how my own philosophy (i.e., my "East Asian" worldviews) shaped my interpretations still remained. This book is in part an effort for me to account for multiple perspectives—Western Science, Native Science, and East Asian perspectives. The first two are relatively well-studied; however, there is no existing work that accounts for an East Asian perspective of archaeological interpretation.

In this vein, this book is an effort to do three things: to share my collaborative research with Native Americans (interpreting Mimbres artifacts and landscape as a case study), to demonstrate how Western archaeological methods shape our understanding of Native American artifacts and landscape, and to account for my Japanese/East Asian worldview. In another vein, this book is an effort to do more, drawing on East Asian philosophy; it is an attempt to correlate the different interpretations as methodology itself, hence the title of the book: *Correlative Archaeology*. To set the stage for this work, I would like to introduce one of my inspirations and an insight that draws on the Japanese practice of Zen Buddhism.

MANY BUDDHAS

There is not much about how being Japanese translates into Western archaeology. As an inspiration, however, I draw upon the work of a Japanese biologist, Tatsuo Motokawa, who thought deeply about what it meant to be a Japanese scientist in a Western context. In his essay "Sushi Science and Hamburger Science" (1989), Motokawa reflects on his experience as a Japanese scientist practicing in the United States by comparing and contrasting Christian and Zen Buddhist worldviews. I offer three of his insights pertaining to ontology, language, and epistemology to help frame my thinking about what it means to be a Japanese archaeologist practicing Western archaeology.

One of the central differences that Motokawa (1989, Figure 2) identified is that while Christianity is monothetic, Zen Buddhism is polythetic. Unlike the one God and one truth of Christian worldviews, in Zen Buddhism there are "many Buddhas" and many paths to enlightenment. Of course, Zen Buddhism still has certain tenets: 1) all manifestations are impermanent (impermanence); 2) attachment is the source of suffering; 3) all phenomena are empty and selfless (nothingness); and 4) peace (Nirvana) is enlightenment. For Japanese, this means that science is an effort to experience the subject or study; in other words, while conducting scientific research, researchers attempt to be with the subject or study. In contrast, drawing on Christianity's view of creation and humanity's domain of the earth, Motokawa (1989, 494) saw one the tenets of Western Science to be that nature is a reasonable and uniform entity that can be discovered through universal rules or patterns. The universal rule exists, and it is created and related to God's will. Under this premise, Western scientists can find universal rules, laws, or patterns in nature if they work hard to investigate them. In contrast, in Zen Buddhism, scientists believe that there are many laws and patterns, and nature is not uniform. Eastern Asians follow this kind of belief and thought because there are many rules, implying that there are many Buddhas in the world.

A second insight that Motokawa offers centers on the epistemic qualities of language. According to Motokawa (1989, 502), the logic of language between West and East is different. For example, Japanese scientists are typically hesitant to state an explicit conclusion (or absolute truth). By stating the truth, it would close our world; in other words, it is contrary to the belief of "many Buddhas" because a single truth limits our perceptions and capacity to interpret meaning (Motokawa 1989, 503). Declaring the truth would hardly ever take place among Japanese scientists because the truth can't be delivered and expressed by words. Instead, Japanese scientists generally attempt to describe one fact or aspect from various points of view and help other scientists to point at some direction. In other words, according to Motokawa (1989, 503), "If we do not state a conclusion and let other people draw the conclusion by themselves, our world is open to others." Therefore, unlike the logic of language in the West which has a structure that each sentence is connected and linearly arranged to reach a conclusion, Japanese scientists follow their logic of language by three-dimensional structure (Motokawa 1989, 502, Figure 6) in which various points of view are surrounding the fact. Simply put, Japanese scientists generally accept many perspectives and interpretations of scientific discoveries because it is built on the philosophy of multiple truths (or many Buddhas).

Finally, Motokawa (1989) also gives important insights into how knowledge is produced and disseminated in the East and West. In the West, scholarship has a currency that is associated with the author's name and institutional affiliations. This practice centers on what Motokawa describes as the Western ego or "I" that possesses and produces knowledge. In contrast, the Zen principles of non-attachment and impermanence focus on trying research as a method of enlightenment rather than possession. This difference fundamentally changes not only the goal of scientific knowledge but also the practice—if knowledge is something that someone needs to take credit for, then that shapes the production, just as if knowledge is something that isn't attached to any one person, that shapes the production.

Of course, one of the biggest differences between my work and Motokawa's is that Native American archaeology adds a third dimension to the dichotomy between the East and West; for example, Native American ontologies, languages, and epistemologies. And one of the goals of this book is to consider how adding a third perspective changes our thinking between West and East and/or West and Natives. In regard to the latter, it is particularly to examine how we look at and interpret artifacts and landscapes. I believe that the concept of "many Buddhas," or, more academically, "correlative thinking," would help facilitate this work. As we will get into in more depth, correlative thinking is a way to make connections between different paradigms, which in some cases complement one another, in other cases conflict with one another, and in other cases question one another.

While some might think that this book is too self-centered and/or not a concern to the field of archaeology, it is important to realize that conversations about identity politics and knowledge productions have been happening in anthropology (e.g., Cheater 2003; Gad et al. 2015; Hodder 1994; Hodder and Hutson 2003; Schneider 2011) and more broadly speaking in the cultural studies (e.g., Fuchs 2009; Tilley 2014) for a long time. In the spirit of post-processual archaeology, which championed discussion of identity and power, it is important to bring this concern to our thinking about archaeological interpretation.

Throughout this book, I will use my Eastern philosophies (mostly Buddhism and Taoism) to inquire and facilitate how North American archaeologists' and Native Americans' perspectives would be improved in archaeological interpretations. I hope that my unique background (i.e., as a United States national citizen who grew up in Japan, practicing Eastern philosophies, and trained as a processual archaeologist) will contribute an alternative way of integrating and correlating diverse archaeological interpretations.

Finally, I hope that this book targets both scholars and students who are interested in archaeology, anthropology, museum studies, Native American studies, and East Asian studies. The concept of correlative thinking can be used as a theoretical framework for numerous disciplines and helps link the results of their discoveries from both humanistic and scientific studies. Specifically, this book will be beneficial for scholars and students in archaeology who are considering and exploring alternative ways of archaeological interpretations and research procedures.

Acknowledgements

The theme of this book originates from two presentations I gave in 2016: *Non-Western Philosophies in Archaeology: Exploring Archaeological Interpretation with East Asian Perspectives* at the Theoretical Archaeology Group Conference, the University of Colorado, Boulder, and *Eastern and Western Perspectives on Archaeology and the Past*, organized by Archaeology Southwest (Archaeology Café) in Tucson, Arizona. When I presented these papers, I was not satisfied with what I really wanted to say about archaeological interpretations using Eastern Asian perspectives, and indeed I felt that my presentations did not make sense for many people in the audience. While I was struggling to organize my thoughts and perspectives regarding the subject, several scholars motivated me to pursue this innovative perspective on the archaeological record. They include Dylan Retzinger (New Mexico State University) and Michael Myers (Washington State University). Without their advice and inspiration (especially Dylan Retzinger's), I would not have been able to clarify my thoughts related to the application of East Asian ontologies to archaeological interpretations of the prehistory of the American Southwest.

This book is the product of three perspectives: Eastern, Western, and Native American. I learned a wealth of Eastern Asian ontologies and metaphysics from Nick Gier (University of Idaho), though when we first met, I could not speak or write well in English while taking his Buddhism, Confucius/Taoism, and Hinduism classes as a new undergraduate student from Japan. On Western perspectives, I thank my dissertation committee at Washington State University, including Tim Kohler (chair), Bill Lipe (mentor), Bill Andrefsky, and Andrew Duff and other faculty members. Comprehensively, I learned how to conduct systematic and empirical research from these scholars. I also thank Mark Varien (Crow Canyon Archaeological Center) and Scott Ortman (University of Colorado) who patiently listened to me and demonstrated options for integrating Native Americans' voices into the archaeological research. I also thank Michelle Hegmon, who has been my mentor and who has published influential materials to facilitate my exploration, allowing me to expand on her ideas and perspectives.

For the Native American perspectives, I thank many people, including Don Pepion (New Mexico State University), Becky Hammond (my older sister), Tessie Naranjo (my mentor), Porter Swentzell, Joseph Suina, and the many Native American advisory groups at Crow Canyon Archaeological Center. Of course, I thank Native American scholars, artists, and elders who helped me conduct multivocal projects, including Jim Enote, Octavius Seowtewa, Gwen Setalla, Gerald Lomaventema, Ed Kabotie, Spencer Nutima, and Ramson Lomatewama. They are my mentors, and they always provide insightful thoughts, feelings, and perceptions about ancient materials and landscapes. I also want to thank Atsunori Ito (National Museum of Ethnology in Japan) and Kelley Hays-Gilpin (Northern Arizona University), who taught me how to conduct collaborative work with Native American peoples, especially Hopi artists. I also thank Chris Adams and Bella Mollard for giving me an opportunity to conduct archaeological research in Gila National Forest.

In terms of publication of this book, I thank John Kantner for asking me to submit my manuscript and Kasey Beduhn for answering many of my questions regarding the format of this book. Chris Nicholson (Arizona State University) has generously proofread hundreds of my documents without asking for any compensation. Finally, I want to thank Momo Arakawa for supporting me throughout this project and in life.

Chapter 1

Rethinking Archaeological Theory

Archaeology is not just a linear analysis of artifacts; it is a complex interpretative process that is determined by an assemblage of vocational training, theoretical lenses, terministic screens, discourse, cultural memory, embodiment, and lived experiences. When we look at an eleventh-century Native American pot, for example, with a four-legged pointy-eared figure painted on one side, one person might interpret it as a dog or a coyote; another might say it represents the trickster or a Native American myth; another might focus on the technique of the painting or the materials of the pot and paint itself; and another might discuss the economic implications of its capacity as a vessel. This is not to say that one interpretation is more accurate or important than another, but a reminder that each artifact is an object of multiple and opaque truths.

With many truths in mind, there are many factors that archaeologists must account for in their analysis. First and foremost, making sense of these different and competing interpretations is not only difficult but also a political and rhetorical act. In other words, discourse is at once a contentious activity by nature (one that invites participants to argue with and debate one another) and a political activity (one that has power structures and institutions that decide who is allowed to participate in the debate). This invites us to ask questions like: How do we create dialogue between different methodologies, and how do we evaluate the ethos of any given methodology? Second, not all interpretations, positions of power, or arguments, for that matter, are equally accessible to all archaeologists (or to other invested interpreters from different fields or walks of life). This reminds us that interpretations are an embodied and material act that have affective dimensions.

Identifying the predicaments of rhetoric and power and institutions and bodies is not intended to unnecessarily complicate analyses or render the interpretation of artifacts impossible. Rather it is to remind us that archaeologists need to account for these different interpretations, and this accounting is a recurring theoretical challenge that scholars have wrestled with for

1

years. As Hawkes (1954, 162) reminds us, archaeological interpretation is especially difficult when we are examining objects associated with religion and spiritual life. Because abstract signs embedded in prehistoric objects and spaces such as pottery designs, rock art depictions, and ritual landscapes are the most subjective matter for archaeological interpretations, it is crucial for archaeologists to find an innovative and alternative perspective, which is the subject of this book.

Drawing on Eastern philosophy and introducing correlative thinking to archaeological analysis, I am attempting to develop a method for complementary interpretations in archaeology, particularly when archaeologists investigate abstract signs which are ubiquitous in prehistoric arts and landscapes. To situate my argument, I provided a narrative regarding my own academic background in the preface and explained where the existential dimensions of my interests came from. If we are going to account for our bodies, experiences, and perspectives in archaeological interpretation, it is important that we locate and account for these dimensions.

Following my narrative in the preface, to locate and situate our investigation, this chapter introduces two case studies pertaining to the interpretation of Mimbres artifacts and landscapes and then surveys competing archaeological and Indigenous methodologies to consider how we might interpret and relate to the same artifacts and landscape from different points of view. Finally, to address issues of paradigmatic division, I introduce correlative thinking, which draws on Taoist philosophy as a methodology for articulating relationships between theories rather than replacing one theory with another.

MIMBRES CASE STUDIES

From 2017 to 2019 I was involved in the Mimbres Pottery Design Workshop with five Hopi artists, and from 2019 to 2020 in the Cultural Landscape Studies in Gila National Forest with two Zuni elders. Although there are more than twenty Native American groups in the American Southwest, I worked with the Hopi and Zuni tribal groups. One major reason is that both the Hopis and Zunis identify with and are recognized by archaeologists as direct descendants of the Mimbres. Both actively participate in federal regulations and policies (i.e., Native American Graves Protection and Repatriation Act) regarding human remains and funerary objects recovered from the land.

For those who are not familiar, "Mimbres" is part of the Mogollon cultural tradition located in southern New Mexico, southeastern Arizona, western Texas, and northern Mexico. The Mimbres occupied the area from AD 1000 to 1150 (Figure 1.1). This culture was assigned the name because many of the sites associated with the Mimbres culture were found along the Mimbres

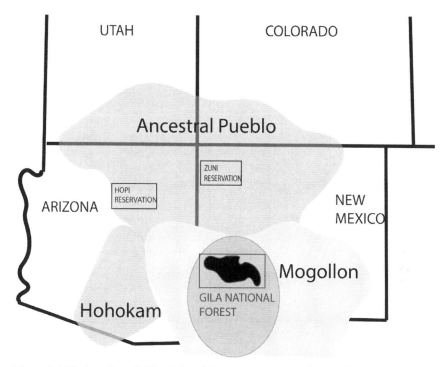

Figure 1.1. The location of Gila National Forest, Hopi Reservation, and Zuni Reservation, showing the Mimbres culture area.

River in southern New Mexico. The name "Mimbres" comes from Spanish settlers, who named the river after the willows (*mimbres*) growing along the banks (LeBlanc 2004; Shafer 2003). Importantly, the Mimbres culture was initially defined by archaeologists in the 1920s and 1930s, and the culture has been affiliated and recognized by many living descendant groups, including the Hopi and Zuni.

In this section, which anticipates Chapters 5 and 6, I will briefly introduce two case studies with Hopi artists and Zuni scholars regarding the Mimbres culture, landscape, and people.

Mimbres/Hopi

The Mimbres Pottery Design Workshop was directed by a Japanese cultural anthropologist, Dr. Atsunori Ito (Principal Investigator), and included five Hopi artists: Ramson Lomatewama, Gerald Lomaventema, Gwen Setalla, Spencer Nutima, and Ed Kabotie. We carried out this workshop as a singular case study for addressing a multivocal approach in collaboration with descendant communities. This workshop took place at the American

Indian Student Center at NMSU and the Geronimo Springs Museum in Truth or Consequences, New Mexico, for four days. Our intention in this workshop was to record the Hopi artists' narratives based on their review of Mimbres pottery designs curated at the University Museum (fifteen pieces) and Geronimo Springs Museum (twenty-two pieces). The majority of these Mimbres pottery vessels were collected by archaeology field schools or donated by residents in southern New Mexico.

These Hopi artists became interested in joining the workshop because they use Mimbres designs and motifs in their artwork; therefore, they feel a connection and affiliation with the Mimbres culture and people. Ito and I began collaborating on this project because our research interests became intersected in 2016. Ito has been interested in the history and culture of Hopi silversmith jewelries and has worked with several Hopi artists for more than fifteen years. He became interested in the Mimbres pottery designs because they were the inspiration for some of the Hopi silversmiths' original designs and motifs since the 1940s, when there was a resurgence in Hopi art (Kabotie 1982). For me, I was interested in eliciting multivocal approaches to archaeological interpretations of Mimbres pottery designs by listening to descendant groups' interpretations of them. Because of these mutual interests, we decided to collaborate on the Mimbres Pottery Design Workshop with five Hopi artists.

Through this case study, the parties involved sought to demonstrate how archaeologists and museum personnel can work with descendant communities by using prehistoric materials to delve into multifaceted and alternative interpretations of ancient designs and motifs. Ito was wanting to record these Native artists' perspectives because there weren't any previous Native perspectives that were documented, and he wanted to preserve their narratives for future generations. While we were recording these Hopi artists' narratives regarding numerous Mimbres pottery designs and motifs, I rendered several observations and impressions about how the Hopi artists reflected on and responded to each other's views and thoughts regarding ancient arts and potters. Importantly, the five Hopi artists generally shared similar thoughts and interpretations about several Mimbres pottery designs, but they also provided different interpretations for some of the designs and motifs. For example, there was consensus on the pottery designs related to the crane, ram, turkey, and fish. However, some of the abstract designs, such as the coyote, horny toad, katsina figure, and bee, inspired multiple interpretations.

When the Hopi artists, for example, reviewed a bee-like insect on a Mimbres bowl, many artists interpreted that the motif in the center represented a bee or some kind of bug, such as a wasp or hornet. Spencer Nutima wondered if it might symbolize a cicada. However, many of them agreed that the geometric (angular five narrow lines) band designs made them think that the insect has just landed in water and the ripples are going out from that bee (or some kind of bug) where it sat. Ed Kabotie thought that the overall painting design indicates pollination, when a bee comes to enjoy the flower. Although the main character of the drawing had multiple interpretations, the overall band design was agreed to by many Hopi artists.

Obviously, their interpretations of numerous Mimbres pottery designs and motifs were fairly different from those made by processual archaeologists, myself included. For instance, when I as an archaeologist analyzed a similar type of Mimbres pottery vessel using my processual training after this project was completed, I described a unique bee-like motif and its pottery bowl in my notes as:

> The paints of this Style III (Mimbres Classic) small bowl consist of an insectoid figure with complex geometric band designs. These band designs include angular five narrow lines, angular two thick lines (or nested chevron triangles), and one thick rim band. There is one narrow line with suspended solid triangular elements. It is obvious to see that the paint of the angular five narrow lines is merged or connected. The proximal end of the insect's body shows a triangular hatcher motif. This small bowl is quite difficult to tell whether the potter polished after he/she added the kaolin slip or not. Also, it is difficult to determine whether or not the paint was polished. One third of the geometric designs inside the bowl show evidence of fire clouds, and two fire clouds outside of the bowl are visible as well. One major crack, located close to the center of the bowl, illustrates that this bowl was reconstructed or restored by someone in the past. The rim form is flat, showing some cracks and use wear. Sand temper was used for this bowl. This is a small hemispherical shaped bowl.

This example demonstrates that scientific descriptions properly illustrate the size and shape of an object and the manufacturing process, such as the use of raw materials and the firing method. However, the description lacks the meanings behind the symbols and motifs, such as people, tradition, and metaphor.

While listening to the five Hopi artists' narratives, I realized how limited my descriptions and interpretations of the particular object were, and I wondered how I as an archaeologist could integrate and combine their diverse interpretations, particularly of ancient arts. Ramson Lomatewama nicely articulates my conundrum, saying that he does not pretend to provide clear answers; he can only offer his answers from his own personal experience in dealing with similar thoughts and ideas. What I understood from Ramson is that other people's interpretations are also reasonable and acceptable, and he is not trying to speak for the Mimbres artists or their intentions. He asserted that each Hopi artist's narrative is valid, and these interpretations are based on one's personal experience and identity and oral stories shared by different clan traditions. On the basis of this experience, I reflected that Ramson and the other Hopi artists were accepting various ideas and thoughts respectfully regarding interpretations of ancient designs and motifs. Ontologically, their perspectives appear to emphasize a relational or correlational perspective.

Mimbres/Zuni

From 2019 to 2020, I directed another archaeological collaborative work in the Mimbres region with two Zuni scholars—Octavius Seowtewa and Jim Enote. The project is titled Cultural Landscape Studies in Gila National Forest, New Mexico. The two Zuni scholars were interested in participating in the project because the physical distance from the current Zuni homeland to the study area in the Gila National Forest is approximately 200 miles, and the Gila is a place that their ancestors likely visited in the past. For example, both Zuni scholars told me that they still come to this area for hunting deer, elk, and turkey. Therefore, they feel that their ancestors would have behaved similarly. Simply put, these two scholars feel strong connections with the people who inhabited the landscape in the past.

The aim of this project was to visit one Classic Mimbres site and two rock art panels with these Zuni elders and listen to their voices and narratives regarding the landscape used by Mimbres people who inhabited the area from AD 1000 to 1150. Before this project began, I anticipated that Native Americans' perspectives are different from how we as archaeologists perceive a particular landscape. As expected, while we were visiting the archaeological site, I witnessed the Zuni elders see nature and the world in a relational way rather than looking at and analyzing it in the systematic way commonly practiced by Euro-Americans. For example, Octavius expressed his thoughts about the connection or relatedness of things, saying,

> Well, they have a connection like I said. When the stars come out, the birds go to sleep; when the birds wake up, the stars go to sleep, so yeah everything has a connection, everything is for a reason . . .. The different cycles, when to plant, when to harvest, are identified with not just the calendar that is out there but how the Zunis understood, like when the vultures are heading south, it's going to be cold. Little things like that have been passed on, and so everything within our physical being and our spiritual being is all connected, so there's not a beginning and an end to all of our ceremonies. Day one goes into the last day and then it starts all over again. (Octavius Seowtewa, personal communication, October 19, 2019)

Landscape studies for archaeologists is an abstract topic for which it is difficult to tease out how ancient people utilized and conceived a particular land. However, the Native Science or Indigenous ways of knowing approach to the interpretation of landscapes by descendant groups like the Zuni elders can offer us equal and/or alternative descriptions and interpretations in comparison with archaeologists' reconstructions. For example, while listening to the Zuni elders' narratives regarding the cultural landscape in Gila National Forest, I recognized that they are connected to their ancestors who lived in the landscape a long time ago. In addition, their perspectives regarding the landscape are deeply allied with the life of cyclical and continuum sequence. These perspectives are immensely different from processual archaeologists (like myself) who see the landscape according to how the environment and resources shape or determine human behaviors based on the concept of predictability and abundance.

Theoretical Implications

Because of these experiences during the Mimbres Pottery Workshop with five Hopi artists and the Cultural Landscape Studies with two Zuni scholars and following the important multivocal developments in American archaeology (e.g., Atalay 2012; Colwell-Chanthaphonh 2010; Ferguson and Colwell-Chanthaphonh 2006), I decided to tackle my own question regarding the acceptance of the strict duality between scientific and humanistic perspectives in archaeological interpretations. In particular, I recognized that investigating abstract designs represented in artifacts and landscapes can offer us correlative or relational interpretations of identity, tradition, myth, worldview, and lifeways in the past. The method for this kind of analysis includes 1) understanding the symbols by looking at artifacts; 2) reconstructing the culture by juxtaposing the interpretations of artifacts to myth, stories, and religion; 3) engaging in the landscapes by reconnecting abstract designs in rock art with archaeological sites; and 4) analyzing the materials from objective and scientific perspectives. In order to show why we need such a dynamic method, I turn our attention to the history of archaeological theories, focusing on the paradigmatic shifts from culture history, processual, and post-processual to multivocal approaches, and then offer Native Science as a counterpoint to Western epistemics.

ARCHAEOLOGICAL THEORIES
IN THE UNITED STATES

Shifting perspectives and interpretations of archaeological remains have been a fundamental part of the discipline since the inception of archaeological theory in the nineteenth century. Three broad paradigms—culture history, processual, and post-processual—have dominated American archaeology

(Preucel 1991). After the post-processual framework emerged and deconstructed processual construction of archaeological interpretations, the multivocal framework as well as the framework of Native Science or Indigenous ways of knowing by Native Americans or Indigenous people gradually came to light in the field. In this book, I will briefly discuss five archaeological frameworks—culture history, processual, post-processual, multivocal, and Native Science—in order to understand and correlate them using correlative thinking. I explore multivocality and Native Science as a competing or alternative approach to archaeological interpretation.

Culture History and Direct Historical Approach

In the early twentieth century, archaeologists were interested in defining culture areas and describing cultural traits, an approach that formed one of the major archaeological paradigms: "culture history." In the American Southwest, archaeologists regularly met with each other and shared what they had found, items such as architectures, pottery, projectile point types, and human remains in their study area. Through these meetings, they defined three major culture areas in the American Southwest: Anasazi (Ancestral Pueblo), Mogollon, and Hohokam (Kidder 1927). Southwest archaeologists still agree on these three major culture areas nearly a hundred years later.

Another important part of how culture history was practiced in the American Southwest was direct historical approach. While American archaeologists were developing culture cores and culture areas, ethnologists visited many Pueblo tribes and engaged in participant observation at Hopi, Zuni, Acoma, and northern Rio Grande Pueblos in the late nineteenth century and early twentieth centuries (e.g., Cushing 1896; Harrington 1916). At that time, ethnologists and other scholars thoroughly considered that the colonial influence would eventually change and eradicate Native Americans' languages, customs, and religions; therefore, ethnologists were anxious to record and preserve Native Americans' traditions.

Since the mid-twentieth century, using the documentation and information collected by ethnologists, Southwest archaeologists have employed a direct historical approach, which investigates the past by working backward in time from the known ethnographic present to the unknown prehistoric past for interpreting ancestral Pueblo archaeology. The direct historical approach emphasizes historical connection between past and present and promises to help with understanding and reconstructing particular culture histories.

Processual Archaeology

Around the middle of the twentieth century, several North American archaeologists responded to the limitations of the culture history paradigm, and the dominant archaeological paradigms shifted. Lewis Binford (1962, 1964, 1965, 1972, 1983) and his colleagues insisted that archaeological research should focus on scientific methods, and the results of archaeological research ought to be understood and interpreted using positivistic perspectives. This paradigm, called "processual archaeology," viewed culture from a systematic perspective and emphasized that society is an adapted organism through culture.

During the 1960s and 1970s, American archaeologists followed Binford and his colleagues' paradigm shift—a shift that was supported and enabled by the development and innovation of new technologies such as radiocarbon, archaeomagnetic, and obsidian hydration methods of dating artifacts. The scientific approach in conjunction with a positivist framework allowed archaeologists to better understand and reconstruct past environments in their study areas. By doing so, archaeologists began emphasizing extrasomatic aspects of archaeological research, as they regarded environment and climate as crucial variables that have shaped or determined human behaviors in the past. For example, when drought occurred in a particular time, these environmental and climate factors caused humans to respond with their own adaptive behaviors. On the basis of this paradigm, ancient people, for instance, might decide to depopulate their base camp or village and move to another area because severe drought occurred.

Post-Processual Archaeology: A Critical Lens on the Processual Paradigm

Ian Hodder, who still today is the leader and advocate of the post-processual paradigm shift from the processual framework, argues that archaeologists need to be more self-critical and include alternative perspectives. By doing so, the frameworks proposed by processual archaeologists, such as "culture as adaptation," can be opened to debate and more inclusive of different interpretations in archaeology. The themes of the debate can be gender, power, ideology, text discourse, rhetoric and writing, structure and agency, history, and more.

For example, several post-processual archaeologists have tackled the involvement and roles of women in the past (e.g., Conkey and Gero 1991). These scholars argue that although half of the population in a society consists of women, women's activities and roles in archaeological interpretations have been ignored, perhaps due to the processual de-emphasis of individuals as agents in ancient society. Hodder insists that openness to various themes in archaeological theories allows us to shift away from objectivity and the evolutionary universality and generality focus that was the focus of processual archaeologists.

Multivocality

In the United States, archaeologists have been conscientiously attempting to find a common ground for archaeological interpretations using both Western science and Native perspectives (Anyon et al. 1997; Duwe and Preucel 2019; Habu et al. 2008; Swidler et al. 1997). Indeed, there is a prolonged history of seeking this common ground for multi-voices or multivocality. Trigger (2008, 190) stated, "Where multiple interpretations of the past have been proposed, the primary duty of archaeologists is to determine to what extent these [scientific and humanistic interpretations] can be combined to produce a more comprehensive understanding of the past."

In the United States, the open dialogue between archaeologists and Native Americans has been improved because numerous archaeologists (e.g., Atalay 2012; Bernardini et al. 2021; Colwell-Chanthaphonh 2010; Ferguson and Cowell-Chanthaphonh 2006; Habu et al. 2008; Hodder 2008) have advocated and facilitated the importance of eliciting alternative perspectives and interpretations in archaeology. Furthermore, the number of consultations between archaeologists and Native Americans has been exponentially increased after the Native American Graves Protection and Repatriation Act (NAGPRA) required American archaeologists to consult with affiliated and federally recognized Native American groups since 1990. After NAGPRA's implementation, there has been a large increase in the number of collaborative projects between American archaeologists and Native American groups (e.g., Duwe and Preucel 2019; Ferguson and Cowell-Chanthaphonh 2006). Finally, the number of Native American and Indigenous archaeologists in the field has also gradually increased, and they have engaged in developing an Indigenous archaeological paradigm and methodology of their own (Atalay 2006, 2008).

By listening to and integrating voices from Native American members, archaeologists can engage in and record firsthand ethnographic documentation. This is a positive aspect in American archaeology because many archaeologists in the United States have heavily relied on late nineteenth-century or early twentieth-century ethnographic records as a frame of reference to understand and reconstruct archaeological interpretations. However, to improve multivocality in archaeology, it is important for Native American (or Indigenous) archaeologists to understand how Native people from different tribes have their own ontologies independent of those held by other tribes. Next, I will define and discuss what Native perspectives are and why these perspectives are crucial for archaeologists to consider and implement into archaeological interpretations.

Native Science or Indigenous Ways of Knowing

Since the early twentieth-first century, several Native American scholars (Cajete 2000; Deloria 2012; Peat 2002) have explicitly advocated for different ontologies and metaphysics that contrast with Euro-American perspectives. These Native scholars are aware that the majority of anthropological and archaeological literature and ethnographic documents were created by non-Native scholars who carried out participant observation with Native groups in the late nineteenth and early twentieth centuries (Cushing 1896; Harrington 1916; Hewett 1906). Since then, anthropologists and archaeologists have frequently used these accounts as a frame of reference to interpret their own findings. Indeed, there was a fairly limited amount of literature written by Native scholars, especially in the American Southwest, until the middle or late twentieth century (Dozier 1970; Eggan 1950; Naranjo 1995, 2008; Ortiz 1969; Swentzell 1991, 1993). In 1990, after the NAGPRA law was implemented, some Native archaeologists (Atalay 2006, 2008; Watkins 2001) began speaking out on their own perspectives regarding archaeological productions and interpretations as well as sharing alternative ways of knowing and understanding the past.

Archaeologists need to further improve the Native Science or Indigenous ways of knowing approach because the dialectic relationship between narratives and oral traditions from Native or Indigenous people and archaeological theories (culture history, processual, and post-processual) by non-Native scholars creates more tensions regarding archaeological interpretations. Adding one more ontology—correlative thinking—would allow archaeologists to enhance interpretation of the archaeological record. In the next section, I will define what correlative thinking means and then discuss how this discourse can be used in archaeological interpretations.

CORRELATIVE THINKING

The history of archaeology, like the history of many other academic disciplines, is characterized by paradigmatic shifts, where one methodology replaces another (Kunh 1962), or the production of parallel bodies of knowledge that rarely interact and/or do not know how to interact because they are too focused on asking and answering their own questions. One of the goals of this book is to rethink methodological replacement and to facilitate interactions between otherwise disjointed methodologies by articulating paradigmatic relationships—and importantly relationships which induce different types of questions in order to facilitate conversation. Drawing on Taoist philosophy, this book introduces correlative thinking as a framework to do this relational work.

"Correlative thinking" was a term coined by the prominent sinologist Joseph Needham in the 1950s. Trying to articulate the difference between Eastern and Western worldviews, Needham (1956) introduced correlative thinking as a counterpart to analytical thinking, which characterized Western ontologies and metaphysics. He stated that correlative thinking is a general propensity to organize natural, socio-political, and cosmological information in highly ordered systems of correspondences.[1] In other words, correlative thinking is a way for Western scholars to articulate the Chinese and East Asian organismic view of the world, where everything is connected with everything else. To better understand the concept of correlative thinking and to prepare for its application to do the work of paradigmatic relation, I turn our attention to Taoist philosophy.

Taoist Philosophy

Taoism is a philosophy and religion rooted in the science of understanding the human experience in the world. It is at once an existential philosophy that recognizes the world as a place of impermanence and change, and an essential philosophy that articulates the world through predictable patterns with fixed principles (Govinda 1981). However, to characterize Taoism as a kind of existentialism or essentialism misses the point—Taoism is best understood in the tension between the two and the movement that results from that tension. The word Tao (道), in fact, depicts the image of a person walking a path and emphasizes the movement (Ming-Dao 1990).

In its simplest translation, the Tao is understood as a way or path that one can follow and understand through direct experiences. In the more complicated practices, Taoists practice the art of divination by interpreting the structural relationship between the symbols of the *I-Ching*, or *The Book of Changes.* To better understand Taoism as it relates to correlative thinking, I turn our attention to the concepts of Yin and Yang and then to the Wuxing, which I draw on as a model for correlative archaeology.

Yin and Yang

According to Hall and Ames (1998, 1), correlative thinking is based on Classical Chinese cosmologies and the Yin-Yang school (yin–negative, dark, and feminine; yang–positive, bright, and masculine). Hall and Ames (1998, 1) stated, "The relative indifference of correlative thinking to logical analysis means that the ambiguity, vagueness and incoherence associable with images and metaphors are carried over into the more formal elements of thought."

Yin-Yang ontology originates from the concept of dialectical and naturalistic schemes, beginning in the fourth or third century BC in China (Jiang 2013, 439). These dialectical and naturalistic schemes were employed to identify alternative patterns of hierarchical relationship. Zhang (1946; Jiang 2013, 442) argued that Chinese logic is different from the Western sense, stating,

> The Chinese do not make definitions (in the Western sense) but only understand the meaning of a word by contrasting it with its opposite. For example, a "wife" is a "woman who has a husband," and a "husband" is a "man who has a wife." (Zhang 1946, 182–83)

In other words, in the concept of Yin and Yang, opposite or contrary forces are complementary, interconnected, and interdependent—where one exists in relation to another through association. Zhang proposed "correlative logic" or "the logic of correlative duality" (1946, 182) as the counterpart of analytical thinking. Whereas analytical logic employs theses, premises, rebuttals, and conclusions to make sense of reality, correlative logic centers on the concept of dialectical or correlative relationships between opposites. In theory, Yin and Yang helps us remember that the concept is not an either/or standpoint, but instead emphasizes a relational process that is complemented by the other perspective, while both entities are also in motion. In order to discuss associations and movement in more structural terms, I turn our attention to the five elements (Wuxing).

Five Elements (Wuxing)

Taoist science is based on the concept of five elements, or the Wuxing: wood, fire, earth, metal, and water. The five elements can be understood both as essences, where each element has abstract characteristics and attributes, and as relationships, where each element relates to another element in predictable patterns of movement. The Taoists used the properties of the five elements to better understand a myriad of phenomena in the physical world and in human experience. The five elements can be applied to science, medicine, music, the culinary arts, martial arts, and—as I'll propose—to archaeological methodologies. In order to prepare us for my usage of the five elements as a basis for correlative archaeology, I offer a closer look at the Wuxing as structural movements and symbolic associations.

Movement

There are three articulated relationships or cycles among the five elements that can be understood as different kinds of movements: generative, destructive, and demeaning. The generative cycle focuses on how one element produces another: metal generates water; water nourishes wood; wood feeds fire; fire creates earth/ash; and earth bears metal. This cycle helps us understand how one entity, be it a material or idea, gives rise to another in a creative manner. In contrast, the destructive cycle articulates how one element overcomes another: fire melts metal; metal chops wood; wood breaks up earth; earth absorbs water; and water extinguishes fire. This cycle shows us how one entity can dominate another in a different context. Finally, there is the demeaning cycle, in which one element insults or questions the integrity of another: wood dulls metal; metal pokes at fire; fire disrupts water; water muddies earth; and earth degrades wood. This demeaning cycle reminds us that relationships are not always resolved as complementary, on an either/or basis; there can be a third variable with multiple permutations.

In addition to understanding the three cycles or movements, it is important to remember that each element is a symbolically rich concept with different associations in different contexts.

Association

When we look at the elements as symbolic representations, we are reminded that each element is an associative concept and not the word for the element itself. Fire, for example, is not just the phenomenon of a flame—it is the color red; it is a passionate emotion, the southern direction, the planet Mars, a rising martial arts movement, and so on. Fire is a concept that can be applied to anything that exhibits these qualities. Further, in studying the symbolic representations, it is important that we do so in a particular context in order for them to have meaning. When looking at the human body and health, for example, each element corresponds to a Yin and Yang organ; when focusing on a particular sense, such as sight, hearing, or taste, each element correlates to a specific color, sound, or flavor.

The symbolic application also extends to the physical world, where each element corresponds to a direction or force (Table 1.1). What is important to our understanding of these associative relationships is that each element can be used to articulate qualities and relationships in any given context under investigation. Further, by understanding and investigating the structure, we are able to conceptualize relationships and associations of interacting issues so that we will be able to comprehend a whole picture of a situation.

To bring our thinking about Taoist philosophy to a close, it is important to remember that in principle Taoism is a practice that enables its practitioners to understand and act in accordance with their path. Taoism is practiced by priests, doctors, scientists, government functionaries, members of the military, musicians, artists, and so on. It is an open-ended philosophy that is not limited or defined in its application. I am an archaeologist, and in the spirit of

Table 1.1. The vertical relationship, showing the symbolic representations according to the five elements (adapted from Maciocia 1989).

	WOOD 木	FIRE 火	EARTH 土	METAL 金	WATER 水
Direction	East	South	Center	West	North
Season	Spring	Summer	Long Summer	Autumn	Winter
Climatic Condition	Wind	Summer Heat	Dampness	Dryness	Cold
Process	Birth	Growth	Transformation	Harvest	Storage
Color	Green	Red	Yellow	White	Black
Taste	Sour	Bitter	Sweet	Pungent	Salty
Smell	Goatish	Burning	Fragrant	Rank	Rotten
Yin Organ	Liver	Heart	Spleen	Lungs	Kidneys
Yang Organ	Gall Bladder	Small Intestine	Stomach	Large Intestine	Bladder
Opening	Eyes	Tongue	Mouth	Nose	Ears
Tissue	Sinews	Blood Vessels	Flesh	Skin/Hair	Bones
Emotion	Anger	Happiness	Pensiveness	Sadness	Fear
Human Sound	Shout	Laughter	Song	Weeping	Groan

Taoism, my path has led me to the interpretation of Native American pottery, and as we have seen in this chapter, there are many ways to approach this endeavor. To be sure, and as you have seen, I have my methodological commitments and limitations; for example, I can practice processual archaeology, I can design a multivocal study, but I cannot be a Native Scientist. What I can do, however, is try to understand each methodology deeply and to articulate the relationships between them. This associative and relational work characterized by movement is my application of Taoist philosophy, and for the sake of scholarly alignment, I will use the term "correlative archaeology."

Drawing on the concept of movement, in the conclusion of this book, I will propose correlative methodology as a way of articulating the relationship between the different archaeological methods. Focusing on the associative understanding of the five elements, in the next five chapters, I will explore each of five different methods of archaeological interpretations on their own so that we can thoroughly understand and appreciate each of them as paradigms for meaning-making in their own right.

THE PATH AHEAD

Moving ahead, each of the next five chapters will begin with a vignette-style interpretation of a crane-like design Mimbres bowl based on the methodology covered in the respective chapter. Importantly, because my current research is in multivocal and Native Science, the substantive interpretative research will take place in Chapters 5 and 6. However, in order to make my larger argument for correlative archaeology, I have included chapters on culture history, processual, and post-processual paradigms and offered "performances" of those interpretative theories because I am not able to authentically practice them within the scope of this book. In my performances of each theory in Chapters 2, 3, and 4, I will consider the ways in which each methodology might interpret the same artifact. Although these performances will not align perfectly with and may fall short of the work in Chapters 5 and 6, I hope they do service to the larger argument.

NOTES

1. The concept of correlation is similar to but different from the concept of synthesis. The latter accumulates and eliminates differences into something new; in contrast, the concept of correlation focuses on relationships of associative structure—each entity and element never disappears. By using the correlative perspective, each

interpretation can be reasonable, valid, and relevant so that it maintains its entity and element. When other interpretations appear, each interpretation entangles by seeking relationship and connection of things or interpretations.

Chapter 2

The Development of the Culture History Paradigm

A Case Study from the Mimbres Region

Culture history archaeologists who have encountered artifacts like the bowl below (Figure 2.1) began by looking at several attributes, such as designs (slip and paint) and size and shape of the vessel. In order to make sense of

Figure 2.1. Mimbres pottery curated at the New Mexico State University Museum (catalog number 1980.17.476).

what they saw, they would try to find characteristics that it shared with other pottery recovered from a particular area. Focusing on the zoomorphic motifs, which are unique to the Mimbres culture area, they would determine that it is of Mimbres origin. After they understood the origin of the piece, they would focus on the time when the pottery was manufactured. Because Classic Mimbres pottery has been dated between AD 1000 to 1130 based on tree-ring dates, radiocarbon dating, and pottery seriation, they would determine that the pottery was manufactured, used, and discarded sometime around the early eleventh century. Consequently, the culture history archaeologists would declare that the pottery belongs to the Mimbres branch of the Mogollon cultural tradition in the American Southwest. This knowledge would then be used to broaden our understanding of Mimbres pottery and serve as another point of reference if another unidentified artifact was discovered.

IMPACT OF CULTURE HISTORY

The culture history paradigm is one of the foundational theoretical frameworks of archaeology. In fact, culture history established many of the terms and cultural groups that subsequent paradigms continue to use, or at least debate, to this day. Focusing on the Mimbres region as a case study, this chapter attempts to explain how culture history archaeologists defined Native American cultural groups such as "Mogollon," "Hohokam," or "Ancestral Pueblo." To do this, we will consider the kinds of material remains culture history archaeologists examined to distinguish and define the Mimbres cultural groups and the techniques that they employed to make their determinations. I hope that readers will leave this chapter with an understanding of how cultural groups are defined by archaeologists as well as how these classifications are strictly based on descriptions of cultural units or types in a particular area.

Development of Culture History Approach

Archaeologists from the early to middle twentieth century wanted to learn about the temporal and spatial distributions of artifacts and architectural remains recovered from archaeological sites as well as curated at museum and private collections. To help the reader understand how the culture history paradigm came to be, I discuss the historical development of the archaeological theories from which it emerged and its academic formation as a methodology.

In North America, archaeologists began developing archaeology as its own discipline and attempted to separate it from antiquarian ways of doing excavations and collection acquisitions in the early twentieth century. North American archaeologists devoted their time and energy to defining culture areas, describing material cultures, and investigating temporal and spatial distributions of artifacts and architectural materials. At that time, American ethnologists also sought to document Native Americans' lifestyles and oral traditions. However, the practitioners of ethnological and archaeological approaches were rarely interested in archaeological interpretations. Instead, American archaeologists were interested in defining culture areas and describing cultural traits, called a "culture history" paradigm or approach. The aim was to understand and reconstruct how each ancient group lived in a particular area.

The culture history approach was employed by most archaeologists from the middle 1930s to the early 1960s. This approach came to dominate the field of archaeology in the twentieth century. In this paradigm, culture units, which are conceived of as assemblages of traits (or types) that are widely shared within the culture area, are the primary focus of study. The theories and methods that culture history scholars adhered to were derived from the German-born American archaeologist Franz Boas. Boas (1911) emphasized historical particularism, or the idea that each society is a collective representation of its unique historical past. It was clear to these Boasians that most culture traits are shared among multiple culture units or groups; thus, on a purely cultural level, these units or groups were likely to have fuzzy or arbitrary boundaries. In other words, the question of the boundaries of culture units is usually not clearly discussed by culture history scholars. In general, culture history archaeologists in the early twentieth century employed language group or tribal identification as a basis for sampling. Then, whatever culture traits (like artifacts) that were associated with that "tribe" or "group" were taken as indicative of its "culture."

There are four broad theoretical and methodological characteristics of culture history that define its position within archaeology: normative assumptions, descriptive focus, naïve induction, and diffusion. The normative assumption is to infer that cultural traits are broadly shared by people within the culture units. Culture history archaeologists assume that artifacts are an expression of the norms of a culture or cultural group. Thus, studying artifacts would provide us an understanding of the people who used and made them (Childe 1929, v–vi; Johnson 1999, 16).

Culture history scholars use the term "descriptive" to understand and reconstruct a particular culture. The culture history approach focuses on a description of material culture and higher inferential chronology. Walter Taylor ([1948] 1983, 51) explicitly asserted that the culture history approach was tremendously descriptive. They generally described material cultures by looking at time (tradition) and space (horizon), and then employed a normative approach to classify and identify a cultural group or culture. These culture history scholars strongly focused on how cultural traits, such as pottery, lithics, and architectural remains, differ among culture groups.

Naïve induction means that the analyst's perspective can be only from outside the culture. The analysts are people who do not belong to the culture under study, and they should not try to conceive the function or meaning of artifacts from the point of view of people from that culture. In other words, the culture history scholars emphasized the "etic" perspective which centers on objectivity of human behaviors in the past. The analysts also should be open-minded to other cultures and use no particular theory as a framework from which to speculate or analyze problems. However, analysts are able to theorize from a specific pattern to a broad cross-cultural generalization by means of high-level abstraction.

Finally, the term "diffusion" is used to articulate presumable reasons for culture change in a particular culture. In anthropology, historical processes that are invoked to explain the appearance, loss, and spread of traits include invention, loss, diffusion, drift, and migration. In the culture history paradigm, the concept of diffusion, which means the spreading of tangible objects and/or ideas from one area to others, is the main focus for explaining culture change.

Time-Space Systematics

For North American archaeologists in the early twentieth century who followed the culture history approach, time-space systematics were used to define each culture area. Time-space systematics are ways of classifying and organizing archaeological material (artifacts, architectural remains, and others) into spatial and temporal units. Archaeologists use classification to divide objects into reasonable and meaningful groups or types, and they generally classify tangible and intangible objects by their similarities and differences. Types are the basic units of classification for time-space systematics, and are classes of archaeological artifacts or sites defined by consistent clustering of attributes. Attributes are individual characteristics that distinguish one artifact from another (e.g., size, form, material, and texture). The development of this classification process is called typology.

After archaeologists developed a typology for a particular culture, they were eager to identify patterns in material culture through time and over space. Indeed, archaeologists spent vast amounts of time explaining and accounting for these patterns (Willey and Phillips 1958). A significant part of time-space systematics is understanding and reconstructing phases and components. A phase is defined as a block of time that is characterized by one or more distinctive artifacts. It is the basic unit of time-space systematics, of varying time spans and with a deliberately vague definition. A component is defined as a culturally homogenous unit's stay within a single site. For example, a site containing only one occupation is called a single component site, while one that was reoccupied is termed a multicomponent site.

To better understand the time-space systematics, I use Alfred V. Kidder's development of the Pecos Classification (1927) as an example for defining three major cultural traditions in the American Southwest. Then, I introduce William McKern's Midwestern Taxonomic Method and Harold Colton's approaches as representations of the development of the time-space systematics.

Pecos Classification

In 1927, Kidder organized a conference at Pecos, New Mexico, for archaeologists and ethnologists working in the American Southwest called the "Pecos Conference." The aim of the conference was to synthesize what each archaeologist knew about each site or community and develop a time-space systematics for the American Southwest. This conference resulted in what is now known as the Pecos Classification System. Time-space systematics were used to develop the Pecos Classification System based on pottery and stone tool types, architectural styles, and basketries in southwestern sites. Archaeologists have since used the sequence, with later amendments, to add and revise approximate dates for dozens of sites throughout the Southwest and to determine cultural ties and differences among the Ancestral Pueblo, Hohokam, and Mogollon traditions.

The Ancestral Pueblo (or Anasazi) tradition lies in the Colorado Plateau, including the San Juan, Little Colorado, and upper Rio Grande valleys (see Figure 1.1). The contemporary Pueblo groups and their ancestors have inhabited the Colorado Plateau for about 2,000 years, and they have been relying mainly upon natural runoff from springs and floodplain water to harvest and cultivate their crops, such as maize, squash, and beans. Their villages consist of small or large multistory masonry structures and religious or communal gathering structures known as kivas. Some of these kivas contain mural paintings. The Ancestral Pueblo people manufactured and used black-on-white painted wares, which were mostly used for serving purposes, and plain and corrugated wares, used for culinary purposes. The majority of black-on-white wares were decorated by geometric designs.

The Hohokam tradition developed an elaborate system of ditches to irrigate the desert in southern Arizona, including in the Tucson and Phoenix basins (see Figure 1.1). In terms of decoration of artifacts, the Hohokam people painted, carved, engraved, and even etched both human and animal figures on pottery, stone tools, pallets, and ornaments of stone and shell. Unlike the black-on-white pottery by Ancestral Puebloans, the Hohokam pottery was painted in red designs on a buff background. In addition, the Hohokam people constructed and used large oval courts, in which a ceremonial ball game was possibly practiced and performed. The burial practice of the Hohokam was by cremation, and the ashes were commonly placed in the ground with a number of grave objects.

When Kidder and others attempted to define the Mogollon as one of the culture traditions, they listed a few differences compared to the Ancestral Pueblo and Hohokam (see Figure 1.1). Kidder (1924) asserted that similar to the Ancestral Pueblo people, the Mogollon people relied upon natural runoff of water from the mountain streams to harvest and cultivate their crops. He also identified similarities of simple pithouses, tubular pipes, and ornaments of Hohokam type. However, one major difference pertaining to the Mogollon tradition was the way people buried their dead. In the Mogollon burial practice, people buried their dead unburned in pits or beneath cairns in conjunction with mortuary offerings. Furthermore, the Mogollon pottery was mostly polished, smudged, or painted red on brown. Indeed, the clear distinction of Mogollon tradition from the Ancestral Pueblo and Hohokam was not established until the middle twentieth century.

Midwestern Taxonomic (McKern's) Method

During the 1920s and 1930s in the eastern United States, archaeologists had few sites with a good stratigraphy. Many museums had private collections with little provenience information and a wealth of data from government-sponsored programs like the Civilian Conservation Corps starting in 1933. At that time, McKern (1939) was concerned about the lack of a standardized cultural scheme using all the data that had been collected. To solve this issue, McKern used a "determinant" which denotes any culture trait when used as a marker for any specific cultural division. The determinant depends on what archaeologists are comparing, such as pottery sherds, lithics, or architectural remains.

Influenced by a biological and genetic idea of culture, McKern employed six different terms in his taxonomic system, including focus, aspect, phase, pattern, and base. Focus means a list of traits for a culture. Aspect is a group of similar foci when compared to something else. Phase is a group of similar aspects when compared to something else. Pattern means a group of similar phases when compared to something else. Base is a group of similar patterns when compared to something else. McKern argued that traits should be compared throughout an entire community, not just in spaces used in similar ways (i.e., rock shelters, open habitation sites, upland hunting camps, etc.). To successfully carry out this system, particularly in order to segregate groups,

McKern argued that a multivariate statistical technique (i.e., cluster analysis) was needed.

McKern's classification system is called the Midwestern Taxonomic Method, and it served a useful purpose at the time. It allowed archaeologists to organize their unstratified data in order to answer research questions. However, there are a few weaknesses. First, the method perpetuated the pessimistic view of Native Americans' capacity for culture change by downplaying the influence of diffusion. Second, as more sites in the East were discovered that were stratified, and archaeologists could employ the use of seriation to reconstruct the temporal occupation of archaeological sites, the Midwestern Taxonomic Method went out of date and chronology took its place in the 1960s.

Gladwin Classification and Colton's Model

The Pecos Classification in the American Southwest needed modification because chronological and regional variations existed, particularly southern Hohokam and southwestern Mogollon areas in the Southwest. At that time, Winifred and Harold Gladwin emphasized a chronological and genetic series which was the middle unit of McKern's hierarchy, with phase as the highest unit. This Gladwin Classification (1934) used the analogy of a tree—with roots, stems, branches, and phases—to present a genetic chronological scheme.

When Harold Colton (1939) intended to establish a classification model for northern Arizona, he took into consideration two major models: the Gladwin Classification and the McKern or Midwestern Taxonomic Method. The difference between these two models is that Gladwin's model focused on a chronological and genetic hierarchy of units, each unit differing from the one below by certain traits. On the other hand, the McKern model relied on statistical methods, particularly on calculating the percentage of cultural traits (i.e., comparing two different cultures and calculating what percentage of traits they share) to distinguish five different levels of similarity: focus, aspect, phase, pattern, and base.

Because the Gladwin model dealt with the idea of chronology as well as location, Colton mainly used Gladwin's model. Presumably, Galdwin's model became very useful at the time because the tree-ring method (dendrochronology) was well-developed in the 1930s and helped archaeologists to clearly distinguish periods of time in archaeological sites. However, the Colton model was different from the Gladwin model because Colton combined or supplemented both Gladwin's and McKern's models into one. Colton's classification takes into account time and space and calculates the percentage of cultural traits to reconstruct cultural boundaries. His taxonomic terminology included: component, focus, branch, stem, and root. The term "focus" by Colton was quite synonymous with Gladwin's term "phase."

Like Gladwin (Gladwin and Gladwin 1934), Colton believed that differentiating and relating cultural units could be accomplished by the use of hierarchical taxonomy, and also that these groupings of cultural units could be analyzed for phylogenetic relationships (Colton and Hargrave 1937, 4). Colton particularly viewed pottery typology as the single most important means of distinguishing cultural groups and for dating archaeological sites in conjunction with tree-ring data.

One interesting point is that Colton believed the technology of making pottery wares (the utility wares including cooking and storage jars) is relatively stable and quite genetic, which means not that it is biological but more a historical implication. According to Colton (1939, 20), "Since the basic pottery techniques are handed down from mother to daughter, they are more stable than styles of design which are affected more rapidly by diffusion." This statement may suggest Colton's view that technology or techniques of cultural units change only slightly or gradually but not rapidly. It also conveys that pottery wares may be a great indicator for identifying roots in the hierarchical taxonomy. Colton and Hargrave (1937, 2) listed six characteristics of pottery that are indicative of different cultural types: surface color, method of handling the clay, texture of the core, chemical composition of the temper, chemical composition of the paint, and styles of design in decorated pottery. Then, Colton and Hargrave (1937, 2) defined a ware as "a group of pottery types which has a majority of characteristics in common but that differ in others." On the other hand, Colton suggests that the effects of time, space, and cultural traits—such as pottery types, architecture, stone, shell, fiber, and disposal of the dead—need to be considered when discussing the terms focus, branch, and stem.

In summary, like McKern's and Gladwin's typological development, Colton's contribution to archaeology at the time was to develop a new taxonomic classification for a focus or phase level, employing time, space, and cultural traits to distinguish cultural boundaries in the northern Arizona and other Southwest areas. Because of his contributions, the time-space systematics within the Ancestral Pueblo area were well established in comparison to the Hohokam and Mogollon culture areas. Particularly, the latter was not defined until the 1930s or 1940s.

The Direct Historical Approach in Culture History

While the discipline of archaeology was being developed in the United States around the late nineteenth and early twentieth centuries, a series of expeditions took place, providing opportunities for several scholars to carry out archaeological and ethnographic research in the American Southwest. These individuals became considered the fathers of southwestern archaeology and included Adolph F. Bandelier, Byron Cummings, Frank Hamilton Cushing, Jesse W. Fewkes, Edgar L. Hewett, Water Hough, Cosmos Mindeleff, Victor Mindeleff, and James Stevenson (Cordell and McBrinn 2016).

These early explorers and scholars engaged in collecting archaeological and ethnographic materials for major East Coast museums. While conducting archaeological research, several of these scholars became familiar with Native American groups and integrated ethnographic information to describe and interpret archaeological artifacts they collected or observed. For example, Cushing interviewed and observed the people and culture in Zuni and used them for interpreting the archaeological remains. Fewkes recorded many narratives from Hopi people and used them for interpreting archaeological remains. Fewkes's use of Native narratives to interpret archaeological artifacts is known as the "direct historical approach."

In the early to mid twentieth century, several socio-cultural anthropologists, such as Elsie Clews Parsons (1925, 1929), Mischa Titiev ([1944] 1992), Fred Eggan (1950), Alfonzo Ortiz (1969), and Edward Dozier (1965) continued to conduct their research on linguistic, kinship, and ceremonial organizations in the American Southwest. For example, in the northern Rio Grande region, Ortiz (1969) described and interpreted the important concepts of the four cardinal directions plus the directions of zenith and nadir of the eastern Pueblo worldview. Another example is that while Alfred Kroeber (1916) was researching Zuni kin and clan systems, he also visited archaeological sites in Zuni and published a manuscript of "Zuni Potsherds" based on his systematic analysis of pottery sherds recovered from these sites.

Julian Steward (1937, 1942) was the most influential scholar who attempted to bring together the results of archaeology and ethnology. Steward objected to the dissolution or fragmentation of archaeological and ethnological evidences, saying, "Ethnology tends to ignore the results of archaeology, while archaeology, concentrating on its techniques for excavation and its methods for description and classification of the physical properties of artifacts, comes to consider itself a 'natural,' or 'biological,' or an 'earth science' rather than a cultural science" (1942, 339). He claimed that archaeologists must use ethnography to develop sociological interpretations of archaeological sites, while ethnographers must integrate archaeological evidence to place their organizational claims in historical context (1937).

The direct historical approach is one of the unique approaches in doing archaeological research in North America as well as parts of Latin America. This is because the disciplines of archaeology and anthropology developed as separate and independent in Europe and other countries, like Japan. In the United States, the discipline of archaeology evolved as a historical branch of anthropology and focused mostly on the ancient histories and prehistories of Native American peoples. Although this approach has been embedded in archaeological research in the United States for over a hundred years, the relevance of the direct historical approach has been challenged several times.

In the early twentieth century, as the new science—seriation and absolute dating methods (e.g., dendrochronology)—matured, the direct historical approach was deserted because of its uncritical use of Pueblo oral traditions to link present to past. It became incredibly difficult for archaeologists to separate these facts, such as oral traditions and narratives, from literary and moral elements. In addition, Southwest archaeologists used Pueblo ethnographies in a far more limited and cautious way because of the deep time gap between cultural practices and their associated material culture in the Pueblo present and the material-behavioral relationships of many centuries ago. The concern over the direct historical approach as a useful device for interpreting the archaeological record continued until the late twentieth century.

In the Mimbres region, similar issues pertaining to the direct historical approach concern archaeologists. Mimbres archaeologists have often found it difficult to tease out whether they should use ethnographic and ethnological information derived from Hopi, Zuni, or Acoma, or the combination of one or two. In addition, applying information collected from sources in the late nineteenth century and early twentieth century to the Mimbres people and societies existing 700 to 800 years ago would not provide accurate interpretations. In other words, there might not be direct continuity between historically documented communities and the prehistoric occupants of many Southwest areas.

Because of these reasons, the direct historical approach had not been regularly employed in archaeological research in the American Southwest until the late twentieth century and the early twenty-first century. In the Mimbres region, the combination of archaeological and ethnological research has not been commonly practiced; instead, archaeologists have focused heavily on chronological development of the region by using scientific methods.

The Development of the Mimbres Culture Area

From the late nineteenth to the early twentieth century, the chronological development of the Mimbres culture area in the Mogollon branch was different from other branches, such as Ancestral Pueblo and Hohokam (LeBlanc and Whalen 1980). This was due to the lack of the extraordinary ruins and elaborate ceramic complexes which attracted early explorers and archaeologists at that time. According to Fewkes (1914, 2), "The valley of the Mimbres has never been regarded as favorable to archaeological studies, but has practically been overlooked, possibly because of the more attractive fields in the regions to the north and west, so that only very meager accounts have been published." However, there were several scholars who discussed and conducted archaeological research in the Mimbres and surrounding areas. For example, U. Francis Duff (1902) discussed archaeological sites near Deming and the lower Mimbres River Valley; Jesse W. Fewkes (1914, 1915, 1916, 1923, 1924) recorded and described pottery recovered from Deming areas; Henry W. Henshaw (1879) reported on artifacts from the Faywood Hot Springs; William Taylor (1898) excavated a large Classic Mimbres site; and Clement L. Webster (1891, 1912a, 1912b, 1913a, 1913b, 1914a, 1914b) investigated several Mimbres sites and excavated the Swarts Site in the Mimbres River Valley area.

From the 1910s to the 1960s, archaeologists became interested in the prehistoric chronology of the American Southwest. The trend was begun by the excavation by Nel Nelson in the Galisteo Basin southeast of Santa Fe in 1914 and by A. V. Kidder's work at Pecos Pueblo in 1915. Since the chronological development was the most important aspect in their research, Nelson and Kidder attempted to obtain a relative chronology by the stratigraphic method. At that time, A. L. Kroeber and Leslie Spier explored and developed the seriation based on different pottery types and attributes recovered from Zuni and other areas. Because of these developments, archaeologists in the American Southwest considered typology, classification, stratification, and seriation as important tools for defining culture areas in space and time. This led to the cultural historical syntheses of regions in the American Southwest.

In the Mimbres River Valley, numerous archaeologists attempted to construct the chronology and culture history of the region using the methods of stratigraphy and seriation. In order for them to achieve the goal, these archaeologists focused on sites that contained over one hundred pueblo rooms with an underlying pithouse occupation. Wesley Bradfield (1929) excavated the Cameron Creek Site; Bruce Bryan (1927a, 1927b, 1931a, 1931b, 1961) and Albert E. Jenks (1930a, 1930b, 1931, 1932a, 1932b) dug the Galaz Site; C. B. Cosgrove and Harriet Cosgrove (1932) worked on the Swarts Site; and Paul Nesbitt (1931) excavated at the Mattocks Site.

Fewkes (1914, 1), who visited the Lower Mimbres area and investigated architecture, artifacts, and settlement patterns in the area, originally recognized that the Mimbres cultural tradition is different from Ancestral Pueblo and Hohokam, saying, "It may be said that while there were many likenesses in their culture, the prehistoric inhabitants of these two regions [Ancestral Pueblo and Hohokam] possessed striking differences, notably in their architecture, their mortuary customs, and the symbolic ornamentation of their pottery." However, Emil W. Haury (1936), who excavated Mogollon and Harris Villages, was the first to assert that the Mogollon culture area should be separated from the Ancestral Pueblo and Hohokam based on the results of his pottery seriation analysis from those pithouse component sites. Furthermore, the Cosgroves' descriptions of archaeological findings, such as architecture, burial practices, skeletal remains, pottery, stone tools, animal bones, and jewelry, recovered from the Swarts Site helped archaeologists develop the culture history in the region (Cosgrove and Cosgrove 1932). Archaeologists working the Mimbres region today continue to rely on the research conducted by culture history scholars from the 1900s to 1960s.

CRITICISMS OF CULTURE HISTORY

Although the approach of culture history in the region is useful for archaeologists today, it is important to consider some limitations of this model. First, the early archaeologists who developed the culture history model mostly conducted their research at over one hundred pueblo structure sites with the most typical structures and artifacts in the Mimbres River Valley. This indicates that small or medium-sized Mimbres sites might display different architectural styles and artifact types. In addition, other sub-regions, such as Upper Gila and Eastern Mimbres, would have different cultural traits, so the cultural boundaries of the Mimbres region would be arbitrary. Finally, while constructing the culture history in the region, early archaeologists did not integrate Native Americans' descriptions and interpretations of these ruins and artifacts. Therefore, there might be a conceptual difference of the ancient culture or culture history when comparing archaeologists' findings and Native American perspectives. As I have indicated some limitations of the culture history in the Mimbres region, I will extend my criticisms of the overall culture history paradigm in the next paragraphs.

The central problem of the culture history paradigm is explaining how historical and psychological processes have operated to form particular culture units. As discussed above, culture units were constructed by a few archaeologists. For example, on the basis of archaeological research done by Bradfield (1929), Bryan (1927a, 1927b, 1931a, 1931b, 1961), Jenks (1930a, 1930b, 1931, 1932a, 1932b), the Cosgroves (1932), and Paul Nesbitt (1931), Haury (1936) synthesized the time-space systematics in the Mimbres region. This classification was developed based on artifact types, architectural styles, and burial practices using seriation and absolute dating methods such as dendrochronology. However, the question of the boundaries of culture units is generally not clearly discussed by the culture history archaeologists. It was clear to these archaeologists (Boasians) that most culture traits are shared among multiple culture units so that on a purely cultural level, the units were likely to have fuzzy boundaries.

A secondary problem is whether culture history scholars can address how humans in a particular society lived in the past. Clyde Kluckhole ([1940] 1972), for example, criticized culture history studies of archaeology by saying that these archaeologists contributed to gathering, analyzing, and synthesizing many archaeological records, but these records do not provide a picture of human behavior in the past. He asserted that archaeology needs to reestablish its scientific method and theory and escape from emphasizing typology. A similar argument was proposed by Walter Taylor ([1948] 1983, 27). He argued that archaeology needs disciplinary structure and needs to be separated from the discipline of history. Both Kluckhole and Taylor suggested that the culture history approach, particularly the methodology of taxonomical classifications, needs to be appropriated to account for dynamics of human behavior in the past.

Steward and Setzler (1938) argued that the lack of understanding of human behavior is due to the lack of functional studies in archaeology. According to their view, "treatment of archaeological objects would be more meaningful if they were regarded not simply as museum specimens but as tools employed by human beings in some pattern of behavior. This requires a deliberate effort to understand their functional place in the total configuration of activity" (1938, 8). Thus, they argued that intensive taxonomic methodologies alone provide a very weak point in archaeology; culture history archaeologists therefore should integrate or synthesize their approach with other configurations.

Finally, it is important to remember that living Native Americans were not consulted by archaeologists in defining these culture groups and areas. The culture history was created by archaeologists in the late nineteenth and early twentieth centuries based mostly on artifact types, architectural styles, and burial practices and their funerary objects by implementing pottery seriation and stratigraphy. Although a few archaeologists and ethnographers interviewed and observed Native Americans' lifestyles and religious practices, the results of archaeological findings and ethnographic documents were not integrated and intersected at that time. This was due to a question about the relevance and reliability of oral traditions and narratives recorded by interviewers of Native Americans to archaeological interpretations. These doubts about the direct historical approach have continued until recently. Because of this background, Native American groups have often been suspicious about how their ancestors' history and prehistory were developed and reconstructed by archaeologists in the past.

Chapter 3

Processual Archaeology

Practicing my training as a processual archaeologist, here is how I would attempt to describe the zoomorphic Mimbres design (Figure 2.1):

Since this is a Style III bowl, it shows the thick kaolin slip with the mineral paint. The polishing process was well done for both the surface and paint inside the bowl, but polishing was not done on the exterior surface. The slip was not also added to the exterior surface, except a little bit of slip showing below the rim. There is no paint on the exterior as well. The rim form is rounded, and detritus and sand temper materials are observed on the rim. Inside the bowl, it shows a little bit of fire clouds. The shape of the bowl is in a hemispherical shape, and it is an excellent condition. This Style III (Mimbres Classic) bowl is a complete or intact vessel. The use wear mainly locates on the rim, approximately 50 percent of the original surface is gone. The bottom of the vase also shows evidence of wear. There are three rim bands; one rim band shows discontinuation due to use wear or just crack. This is a medium-sized Mimbres Classic bowl, having about 18 cm diameter. Since the main design is a bird with a geometric motif (solid diamond element encompassed by a negative diamond element, two hour-glass motifs, and two solid triangles), it is a Style III vessel. The layout of the painted figure locates on the center with three rim bands. These rim bands are narrow width (less than 3 mm). Since this bowl shows evidence of use wear, absence of kill hole, and deposition of non-burial context, unlike a typical Style III Mimbres bowl, this bowl would have been used for utilitarian purposes.

WHAT IS PROCESSUAL ARCHAEOLOGY?

In this chapter, I will briefly define what the processual archaeology paradigm is and discuss how it has developed and been practiced in the American Southwest. In the 1930s, Julian Stewart emphasized the relationship between humans and their environment and how the relationship shapes and determines human behaviors. At that time, ecological modeling and studies of human adaptation to a changing environment had rapidly grown in archaeo-logical research. Due to this movement, innovation in paleoclimatology and geoarchaeology became important components in archaeological research, and this encouraged archaeologists to investigate environmental reconstruc-tion of the past.

The concept of human adaptation to a changing environment further led archaeologists to consider the importance of the structural-functionalist model, which focuses on a synchronic view of culture and examines the relationship between artifacts and their functions within the context of a given cultural group. This trend also helped North American archaeologists address one of the criticisms of the culture history paradigm, which was its inability to explain human behaviors in the past. Willey and Sabloff ([1974] 1993) claimed that the trend of the 1930s was the Explanatory Period (or Modern Period), when archaeologists developed a concern for context and function while still using a classificatory-historical framework. Since the 1960s, American archaeologists focused their research on using explicitly scientific and objective approaches in order to understand and reconstruct evolutionary generalization and regularities of human behaviors in the past (Preucel 1991). This paradigm, called "processual archaeology," viewed culture through a systematic perspective and emphasized adaptation as the driving force of change.

Processual archaeologists proposed five perspectives that differentiated their approach from that of culture history. First, they espoused an evolu-tionary approach that focused on the technological and economic aspects of culture. Second, they offered a systematic view of culture that focused on cultural variability and its systemic organization. This approach became achievable because the use of computer simulations revolutionized the pro-cess of developing advanced systems analyses in archaeology. Third, they employed an ecosystem perspective which viewed human populations as part of ecosystems. Fourth, to understand and reconstruct variability and general-ity in archaeological research, processual archaeologists stressed the use of statistics and paid special attention to sampling techniques that would permit generalizations from a system view of culture.

Finally, processual archaeologists drew attention to a general scientific approach. This included problem-oriented research, hypothesis testing (espe-cially a formal hypothetico-deductive method), and a positivist philosophical position. According to Merrilee Salmon (1992), the positivist perspective is "the view that knowledge of the world is obtained only through applying the scientific method to experience obtained through our senses." Processual archaeologists believe archaeologists ought to employ the explanatory pro-cedures that are an integral part of the positivist perspective so that they can achieve its goal by following deductive reasoning in nature. By doing so, deductive reasoning predicts specifics based on application of general laws.

The "scientific" and "objective" research in conjunction with hypothesis testing was the foundation for the processual archaeological paradigm. Lewis Binford (1962, 1964, 1965, 1972, 1983) insisted that archaeological research should focus on scientific methods, and the results of archaeological research ought to be understood and interpreted by positivistic perspectives. In the next section, I will review how Binford, the advocator of processual archaeology, reached the point that he considered the important paradigm shift in archaeological theory.

ADVOCATOR OF PROCESSUAL
ARCHAEOLOGY—LEWIS BINFORD

Lewis Binford (1972) was frustrated with the general field of archaeology, particularly archaeological study under the culture history paradigm. His major concern with the discipline of archaeology was finding how archaeology could contribute to the general field of anthropology. He considered the major reason that archaeology had not contributed to anthropology was that it did not provide any explanations helpful toward understanding human behavior. He believed an explanation in archaeology should be set within a socio-cultural systemic context (framework), so that archaeology could explain the process of cultural change and evolution. Furthermore, Binford agreed with Leslie White's definition of culture, which is "the extrasomatic means of adaptation for the human organism" (Binford 1962, 218; White 1959, 8). Binford saw culture as an adaptive system, with technology, subsistence economy, and social organization the most significant aspects of the culture (Keesing 1974).

Binford particularly placed emphasis on analyzing technology in a functional context. He identified three general functional classes of artifacts—the technomic, sociotechnic, and ideotechnic—as important for archaeologists to study. He defined technomic as "those artifacts having their primary functional context in coping directly with the physical environment" (Binford 1962, 219). One good example would be finding a mastodon pelvis with a Folsom point in a site. The Folsom point is a technomic artifact since the function of the point is hunting, and it is also associated with the animal.

Binford defined sociotechnic as "artifacts where the material elements hav[e] their primary functional context in the social subsystems of the total cultural system" (Binford 1962, 219). The function of sociotechnic artifacts is to identify and articulate individuals one with another. A great example is a Mimbres black-on-white pottery. If sociotechnic artifacts show changes in the technique of the pottery, we should consider that this may have been caused by social factors, such as increasing population density, competition, and warfare.

Finally, Binford defined ideotechnic in this way: "Items of this class have their primary functional context in the ideological component of the social system" (Binford 1962, 219). Those artifacts are mainly used for symbolic purposes. Some examples are "figures of deities, clan symbols of natural agencies etc." (Binford 1962, 220).

With regard to the adaptive system, Binford claimed that archaeologists are able to understand those general functional classes of artifacts if they look at findings and placement of artifacts as a whole. Binford also stressed that to achieve this understanding, we can make some inferences by looking at these three functional classes of artifacts using deductive reasoning and hypotheses (Willey and Sabloff [1974] 1993, 224).

During the 1960s and 1970s, many North American archaeologists did follow Binford and his colleagues' paradigm shift. This shift was also supported by the development and innovation of new technologies, such as radiocarbon and archaeomagnetic dating as well as obsidian hydration methods. The scientific approach in conjunction with a positivist framework allowed archaeologists to better understand and reconstruct past environments in their study area. By doing so, archaeologists began emphasizing extrasomatic aspects in which environment and climate are regarded as crucial variables that have shaped or determined human behaviors in the past. For example, when drought occurred in a particular time, these environmental and climate factors were seen as causing humans to respond with their own adaptive actions and behaviors. On the basis of this paradigm, ancient people, for instance, might decide to depopulate their village and move to another area because of the severe drought.

MIMBRES AS A CASE STUDY

In the Mimbres area, many processual archaeologists have engaged in research using positivistic and objective perspectives to understand the past. Instrumental to this work has been the Mimbres Foundation, a nonprofit organization established by Steven LeBlanc and his students and colleagues in the 1970s. The major aim of the Mimbres Foundation's work was to investigate the prehistoric occupation of the Mimbres region and to preserve archaeological sites as well as regain artifacts that had been looted.

Much of the Mimbres Foundation's work was conducted using the processual paradigm because the founding members of the foundation identified themselves as processualists. For example, several archaeologists (Anyon et al. 1981; Creel 2006; Gilman and LeBlanc 2017; Nelson 1999; and Shafer 2003) reconstructed settlement patterns and village formations in relation to climatic and environmental changes in the Mimbres River Valley from AD 900 to 1150. In the following sections, I will delve into the theoretical backgrounds of these scholars and then discuss how the processual paradigm in the Mimbres region has been practiced by a few prominent archaeologists.

Theoretical Development in the Mimbres Region

Exploring the backgrounds of prominent archaeologists who influenced archaeological theories and methods in a particular study area allows us to understand how past human societies, cultures, and people in that area have been interpreted. In the Mimbres region, Steven LeBlanc has been the leading and most influential archaeologist since he helped establish the Mimbres Foundation in the 1970s. LeBlanc received his doctoral degree from Washington University in St. Louis, and his dissertation chair was Patty Jo Watson. Watson was one of the prominent archaeologists who stressed the importance of the scientific method in archaeological studies, and she supported the processual paradigm. Although her archaeological research focused on the Near East as well as the eastern United States, Watson helped to codirect the Cibola Archaeological Research Project from 1972 to 1974. Her work at Cibola was primarily focused on investigating a large pueblo site related to the Zuni nation, and she set the standard for testing hypotheses concerning ceramic production, decoration, and evolution within complex New World communities.

In collaboration with Watson and Charles Redman, who was also an advocate for scientific studies and for the processual paradigm in archaeology, LeBlanc published an instrumental archaeological theory and method book, *Archaeological Explanation: The Scientific Method in Archaeology*, in 1971. In the book, they argued that the philosophy of science is highly beneficial for archaeologists, in that archaeologists ought to observe and describe regularities that can be incorporated into theories useful for the explanation and prediction of the phenomena being investigated. Simply put, they persuaded archaeologists to carry out archaeological research empirically, and the hypothetico-deductive method was crucial for them. In the preface of the book's second edition, Watson et al. declared that the deductive method requires that "the conclusion of a deductive inference [should contain] no more information than do the premises, and the conclusion [must follow] from the premises with logical certainty. If the premises are true, the conclusion must also be true" (1984, 5).

LeBlanc as well as his colleagues and students, particularly archaeologists who worked for the Mimbres Foundation, continued to advocate for scientific research, including empirical generalizations and logical reasoning. The Mimbres Foundation developed the investigative framework for carrying out current research in the Mimbres region and beyond since the 1970s. In the late 1960s and early 1970s, the New Archaeology, or processual archaeology (e.g., Watson et al. 1971), was not only stirring up archaeological method and theory, but was also generating new institutional approaches to doing archaeology.

The Mimbres Foundation was a great example of this. For the foundation, field research was a main activity, including both regional surveying and substantial excavations. This was due to the severe destruction of Mimbres sites in the region by looting and pothunting activities for over a hundred years, and it was also based on LeBlanc's emphasis on the processual framework—understanding and reconstructing the nature of the prehistoric occupation through empirical observations and logical reasoning. LeBlanc (1983, 16) said,

> There was little use in working on the internal structure of a single site. Instead, the study of the relationships between sites seemed to be a more fruitful approach. It required the systematic survey of large areas, both to locate sites to excavate and to help understand how they were related to each other. Fortunately, such an approach allowed us to analyze the settlement patterns of the region and the fluctuations in population over time.

LeBlanc managed to recruit field personnel of very high quality, such as Patricia Gilman, Paul Minnis, Roger Anyon, Ben Nelson, and Margaret Nelson, among others. As a group they learned from LeBlanc and became part of the expansion and continuation of his vision. The vision encompassed an innovative conservation strategy; advocacy to strengthen laws to protect archaeological sites; and research, publication, and expansion of the Mimbres pottery database. Indeed, many of the field crew used Mimbres materials in subsequent MA and PhD degrees. Many from those early crews have continued to work in the Mimbres region and have brought their students into the research area. Therefore, I believe that the majority of these archaeologists continue to follow LeBlanc's vision as well as the processual archaeology framework for their research.

Other Mimbres Archaeological Work Using the Processual Archaeological Framework

Archaeological research in the Mimbres region has undergone a different historical trajectory in regard to methodological and theoretical developments compared to archaeological research in the Ancestral Pueblo and Hohokam areas. Two major reasons might account for the differences. One is that numerous Mimbres sites have been severely looted and disturbed by pothunting activities since the early 1900s. This caused Mimbres archaeologists to develop a master database in the region. Second, there was no large-scale Cultural Resource Management (CRM) project, such as a dam or highway construction, from the 1960s to 1980s in the region. Unlike other areas in the American Southwest with major CRM projects (e.g., Dolores Archaeological Research, Cochiti Dam Project, and Interstate 10 construction in Tucson and Phoenix) that provided funds and opportunities enabling archaeologists to develop a rich archaeological database, Mimbres archaeologists have needed to develop their own database by conducting university field schools and small contracted CRM projects.

While carrying out these archaeological studies, the majority of Mimbres archaeologists spent vast amounts of time developing culture histories at particular sites, and they employed the processual framework to understand and reconstruct settlement patterns, the fluctuations in population, and inter-and intra-exchange of artifacts. For example, Harry J. Shafer at Texas A&M directed a long-term excavation at the NAN Ranch Ruin (2003), and Margaret Nelson and Michelle Hegmon at Arizona State University carried out the Eastern Mimbres Project (2010). I will briefly describe each case study and address the theoretical frameworks used.

NAN Ranch Ruin

Harry Shafer conducted two decades of excavations and research at the NAN Ranch Ruin in southwestern New Mexico. The research provides new information on and interpretations of the rise and disappearance of the ancient Mimbres culture that thrived in the area from about AD 600 to 1130. The major contribution of the project was to provide evidence of the introduction of irrigation agriculture in the late ninth century. According to Shafer's study (2003), the change of subsistence patterns was visible in architecture, mortuary practices, and ceramic decoration. The NAN Ranch project has yielded the largest body of evidence ever gathered at a single Mimbres site, so it offers the clearest picture to date of who the ancient Mimbres people were. On the basis of the NAN Ranch project, Shafer clearly traced the occupation of the NAN Ranch site from Pithouses to Mimbres Classic, and then to abandonment around AD 1130.

Shafer reconstructed the Mimbres people's social customs, subsistence, biological information, and the symbolism of the distinctive Mimbres designs in their ceramics, stone artifacts, and jewelry. The aim of the NAN Ranch project was to understand the settlement patterns, the occupational history, and sociopolitical organization from the Pithouse to Mimbres time periods.

Although Shafer tried to understand these aspects using the processual archaeology paradigm, he also argued that the change of settlement patterns in the Mimbres region was reflected in the change of symbolic and ideological implications that occurred during the transition period around the tenth century (1995, 2003). This indicates that although Shafer's interpretations were based on firmly objective and positivistic perspectives, he also considered cultural and social changes of a society from an ideational perspective as well.

Eastern Mimbres Project

In the 1990s, Margaret Nelson and Michelle Hegmon at Arizona State University directed a long-term archaeological field school in areas in the Mimbres region between the east in the Black Range and the west on the Rio Grande. They defined their study area as the "Eastern Mimbres" region. According to Nelson and Hegmon (2010), the majority of sites in which they conducted surveys and excavations were small hamlets or habitation sites dating mostly from Classic to post-Classic periods. On the basis of their findings regarding small habitation sites after AD 1130, they argued that the Mimbres people went through a cycle of dispersion.

Nelson and Hegmon applied the "resistance theory," which originated from processual paradigms. The resistance theory strives to explain the ecological resilience, transformation, and succession that takes place within a system. The specific type of cycle used along with the theory is referred to as an adaptive cycle (Figure 3.1; Gunderson and Holling 2002). This cycle is one that involves four different stages that act as variables in the system. The four stages consist of exploitation (r), conservation (K), release (omega), and reorganization (alpha) (Redman 2005, 73). From exploitation to conservation, the system is in a period of growth, which continues until the carrying capacity—the maximum level of sustainable resource exploitation within an ecological system—of the system is finally maximized, and then the level of resources is no longer sustained by the agents in the system. Conservation to release includes the decline of the carrying capacity in the system to the point where there is enough of a balance to reach reorganization. Reorganization takes place when the carrying capacity of the system has recovered from the decline and can begin to move through the full cycle again (Redman 2005, 73).

Nelson and Hegmon (2010; Nelson 1999) considered that the Mimbres culture can be seen as a system. From the Pithouse to the post-Classic periods, archaeologists can discern which stage of transformation within a system the Mimbres people in each time period went through. To comprehend the stages, archaeologists tried to reconstruct the fluctuations of population,

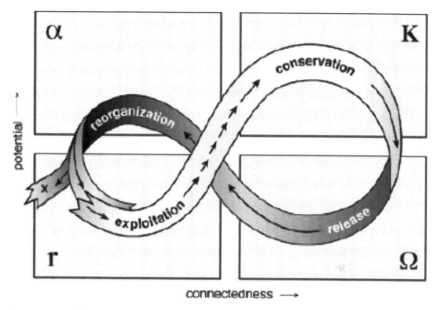

Figure 3.1. Resilience theory adaptive cycle.

abundance or scarcity of resources, and the variability of environmental and climate changes. On the basis of Nelson and Hegmon's research, it is clear that their theoretical and methodological approaches followed the processual paradigm—the consideration of the adaptation and alteration of culture by environmental, demographic, and resource variables.

CRITICISMS OF THE PROCESSUAL ARCHAEOLOGY PARADIGM

Although the processual paradigm is still practiced by many North American archaeologists today, there are some limitations to their archaeological interpretations. First, this paradigm de-emphasizes the historical specifics that the culture historical paradigm stresses. Second, it downplays the importance of the individual in a society. Under the processual paradigm, individuals or agents in a society have limited social and political power, such as in the process of decision making and individual influence on cultural or social change in the past.

Third, although this framework produces effective and useful archaeological data as well as its descriptions and interpretations, the emphasis on positivistic and scientific perspectives has caused American archaeologists to exclude information and ideas from descendant groups who inhabit many areas in the United States where archaeologists have carried out the majority of their research. In other words, Native Americans' perspectives have not been integrated under the processual paradigm. This has led to the strict divergence between archaeologists' and Native Americans' perspectives regarding the reconstruction of the past.

This has further caused diversifying and branching out of more theories and methods from the Native Americans' and processual archaeologists' perspectives. For example, the processual archaeological paradigm helps archaeologists branch out evolutionary perspectives into more particular theories, including human behavioral ecology, evolutionary ecology, and dual inheritance theory. For Native American perspectives, although North American archaeologists have explored and improved multivocal approaches for their interpretations of archaeological record (e.g., Bernardini et al. 2021; Ferguson and Colwell-Chanthaphonh 2006), there are a just few integrations of the results between archaeological research by processual archaeologists and Native Americans' voices and narratives.

In the next chapter, I will introduce the objections to strictly scientific approaches in archaeology that emerged around the 1980s in the United States. This new trend is called the post-processual paradigm, and it focuses on a wider range of issues and encourages archaeologists to accept diverse archaeological interpretations.

Chapter 4

Post-Processual Archaeology

When post-processual archaeologists attempt to describe and interpret a pottery design, they start by trying to collect more data. They would want to interview the archaeologists and field school students who excavated this bowl. They would seek out and try to interview descendant groups who have strong connections and affiliations with the Mimbres culture. They would also broaden their research to include data from other scholars, such as biologists, zoologists, or art historians, for their expertise on animals or arts. Some might even try to gain the insights from members of the general public who might want to express their art appreciation, thoughts, and feelings toward the design and shape of the bowl.

Other post-processual archaeologists might focus on critiquing the existing interpretations by examining the potential for gender or cultural biases and oversights. For example, they might interpret the crane-like figure as a female due to the size and shape of the bird design (Figure 2.1). Others might also say that the geometric designs inside the bird's stomach indicate the idea of the clan or moiety system. At the core of the post-processual paradigm is the belief that the post-processual archaeologist should seek to understand and document the diversity of interpretations.

WHAT IS POST-PROCESSUAL ARCHAEOLOGY?

In the 1980s, North American archaeologists became influenced by European thoughts on archaeological interpretations that challenged the mainstream objective and scientific approaches, such as ecological evolutionary and positivistic perspectives. These archaeologists began focusing on a wider range of issues, including gender, power, ideology, text, discourse, rhetoric and writing, structure and agency, and history (Hodder 1991). This paradigm, titled "post-processual" theory, responded to the limitations of the processual paradigm by rejecting the search for universal laws and regulations.

Post-processual archaeology also rejected the systematic view of culture and emphasized ideology, ritual, symbolism, and archaeology that considers individual agency as part of the interpretative process. Furthermore, post-processual archaeologists insisted on the importance of taking debates in these other disciplines into consideration when developing archaeological methods and interpretations. Finally, post-processual archaeologists also argued that it is difficult to conduct archaeological research with pure objectivity, and this should not be the goal. By and large, the post-processual paradigm was a critique of archaeological interpretations proposed by processual archaeologists.

In this chapter, I will survey the development of the post-processual paradigm and its contributions to the practice of archaeological interpretation. And in the spirit of post-processualism, I will supplement our study of the Mimbres culture by considering how an ethnologist, art historians, folklorists, and a Native American artist have described and interpreted Mimbres pottery designs and motifs from the 1920s to today.

ADVOCATOR OF POST-PROCESSUAL ARCHAEOLOGY—IAN HODDER

Ian Hodder, a British archaeologist, was one of the pioneers of the post-processual movement. He argues that archaeologists need to account for gender, power, agency and structure, and ideology in their methodologies and analysis. To be sure, Hodder was trying to move archaeologists away from the notions of objectivity and evolutionary universality that were championed by processual archaeologists. Hodder (1991, 37) said,

> We are beginning to see in archaeology a rise of different perspectives so that the old dogmas about culture as adaptation, archaeology as anthropology or objective science, have become contested ground. That openness to debate and diversity is what I would call post-processual archaeology.

He further argues that the post-processual framework includes aspects of processual archaeology (later termed "processual plus" by Hegmon), but only within the context of a wider debate on scientific methods. Simply put, Hodder argues that there are different ways of doing science, and different types of problems need different types of argument.

In terms of the methodology, Hodder and other post-processual archaeologists have applied a "hermeneutics" approach, the science of interpretation, to archaeological research. For Hodder, hermeneutics are a way to discover hidden meanings of sacred texts. Hermeneutics involves understanding the world not as a physical system but as an object of human thought and action. Thus, scientific explanation is only one of many methods of understanding. Hodder (1991, 33) elaborates on Gadamer's original definition of hermeneutic, saying,

> The primary hermeneutic rule is that we must understand any detail, such as an object or a word, in terms of the whole, and the whole in terms of the detail. As an interpreter one plays back and forth between part and whole until one achieves the harmony of all the details with the whole. An understanding of the meanings of a situation is thereby achieved.

Drawing on the work of Hodder and other post-processual archaeologists, several North American archaeologists have engaged in gender, agency and structure, and processual-plus approaches. I will discuss each theoretical approach in the following sections.

GENDER STUDIES

In response to the post-processual movement, North American archaeologists attempted to diversify the range of perspectives in archaeological interpretations in the 1980s. One of the prominent developments pertaining to archaeological theories and methods was the subject of gender studies. Since the publication of Conkey and Spector's article titled "Archaeology and the Study of Gender" in 1984, numerous books, edited volumes, and articles pertaining to gender in archaeology have been published (e.g., Barber 1994; Bertelsen et al. 1987; Claassen and Joyce 1997; DuCros and Smith 1992; Ehrenberg 1989; Gero and Conkey 1991; Marshall 1998; Moore and Scott 1997; Walde and Willows 1991).

In 1991, Gero and Conkey published an influential edited volume entitled *Engendering Archaeology: Women and Prehistory*, in which they explicitly stated, "In archaeology, we can 'use' gender to 'do' more and to 'say' more; gender can illustrate the ways in which particular roles and relationships in societies are constructed" (1991, 12–13). Gero and Conkey argue that the study of gender can be a valid, central, and important concept in archaeological research, and that this concept helps us consider the individual as an active social agent. Using the lens of gender, archaeologists can offer an alternative way of answering and interpreting archaeological findings, and they can challenge processual archaeologists' interpretations that relied on objective and scientific methods.

Because of the gender studies movement, several archaeologists began to systematically identify an androcentric bias in the interpretation of the archaeological record (e.g., Gero and Conkey 1991). These studies high-lighted a clear pattern in which men were visible in archaeological interpreta-tion and women were, by and large, invisible. For example, the androcentric bias was particularly prevalent in the interpretation of stone tools, which were, for the most part, interpreted as being associated with male activities (Gero 1991). Critiques of the androcentric bias in archaeological interpreta-tion resulted in new analyses that sought to engender the past and develop methods to identify whether specific activities and uses of space were con-ducted by men or women (Arakawa 2013; Gero and Conkey 1991; Hegmon et al. 2000; Sassaman 1992).

Methodologically and theoretically, archaeologists who considered the importance of gender studies in archaeological interpretations contested how the processual paradigm (positivism) was limited to exploring only concepts including population pressure, resource stress, or sociotechnic subsystems. Instead, archaeologists who advocated gender studies asserted the importance of internal structuring analysis in archaeological research.

AGENCY AND STRUCTURE (PRACTICE THEORY)

Following gender studies, practice theory allowed archaeologists to reex-amine the biases and assumptions in records and interpretations that had previously shaped the discourse. Responding to the presumed objective gaze of social and anthropological paradigms, Pierre Bourdieu, a French sociolo-gist, presented practice theory as a methodology for ethnographic fieldwork that accounted for culture as a dynamic rather than mechanical apparatus (Bourdieu 1977, 72; Moore 2009). Bourdieu argued that culture was a social construct created and determined by the agency of individuals who are actively making decisions in time rather than following external and atempo-ral rules (Bourdieu 1977, 72; Moore 2009).

In more technical terms, practice theory presented archaeologists with a way to rethink the assumptions that they and previous scholars had made about culture by recognizing that cultural remains were created by people who were in conversation with other people in a habitus. For Bourdieu, a habitus was understood as the thoughts and actions that formed cultural pat-terns over time (Moore 2009, 334; Varien and Potter 2008, 7). Key to the idea of a habitus is that it provides understanding and a way to discuss how cultural patterns inform the thoughts and actions of individuals or agents.

Numerous North American archaeologists, especially those whose research has focused on the American Southwest (e.g., Hegmon et al. 2000; Potter 2000; Schachner 2001; Varien and Potter 2008), have followed and used prac-tice theory in their research. Indeed, practice theory might not be a theory, but a way for archaeologists to pay attention to how social structures and agents interacted (Hegmon 2000). According to Hegmon et al. (2000, 43–44),

> Practice theory reminds us that people are not automatons, mindlessly filling their assigned roles (see Connell 1987). Instead, people often do things for specific reasons, and their actions have intended as well as unintended consequences.

For archaeologists who undertake practice theory, both agency and structure ought to be considered when they attempt to interpret their archaeological records. According to Giddens (1984, 9), agency refers to the capability people have for doing things. Agency is a process by which people reproduce, reinforce, and change structure. Therefore, cultural change can take place from within; it does not always have to be precipitated by outside forces as processual archaeologists emphasize with the notion of extrasomatic forces. Structure is something more than a sum of people's day-to-day activities. Theoretically, archaeologists should be able to reconstruct structure by focusing on how people represented and organized their lives, by analyzing evidence such as mortuary practices, material symbolism, and the arrangement and construction of architecture. As Hegmon (2008, 230) stated, "Agency has the potential to humanize archaeology (including both scientific and humanistic traditions) by putting people back into the picture."

MICHELLE HEGMON'S "PROCESSUAL PLUS" APPROACH

Michelle Hegmon (2003) noted that while the majority of North American archaeologists have been open to post-processual perspectives and insights, many archaeologists (especially those who focus on evolutionary ecology, behavioral archaeology, and Darwinian archaeology) have resisted or at least had more difficulty letting go of their scientific (i.e., positivist) commitments. Recognizing the concerns of processualists, Hegmon argued that North American archaeologists should employ a broad array of approaches which she called "processual plus." She noted that although North American archaeologists have leaned toward identifying themselves as processual archaeologists, they have indeed incorporated several concepts—meaning, agency, and gender—in their interpretations of archaeological records. Unlike theoretical developments in Europe where the distinction between processual and post-processual paradigms are clear, Hegmon (2003) argues that North American archaeologists have been blending processualism and post-processualism in order to understand the relationship between structure and agency within a particular community, society, or culture.

Hegmon further argues that North American archaeologists should put their theoretical egos to the side and try not to become attached to any particular approach. By doing so, they will be able to remain open to multiple ways of viewing the past (Preucel 1991; Trigger 1989, 369). This theoretical insight creates a space for North American archaeologists to develop and delve into a conversation informed by multiple perspectives that include processualism.

MIMBRES CASE STUDIES (AGENCY AND STRUCTURE AND PROCESSUAL PLUS)

In the Mimbres region, post-processual archaeological research has not been widely practiced. This is due to the severe looting of archaeological sites and the absence of large CRM projects in the Mimbres region as I discussed in Chapter 3. However, there are two subjects that Mimbres archaeologists have undertaken their archaeological interpretations using post-processual approaches, especially focusing on the concept of agency. One is gender studies using practice theory (Hegmon et al. 2000); the other focuses on individual Mimbres artists (Hegmon and Kulow 2005; LeBlanc 2004). I will explore these case studies as representations of post-processual perspectives and interpretations in the Mimbres region.

Hegmon's Gender Studies (Practice Theory) in the Mimbres Region

Archaeological interpretations on gender topics were addressed by Hegmon and her colleagues' (2000) study of architectural and artifact remains in the Mimbres study area. They employed practice theory, emphasizing the structure and agency of both women and men, and investigated the status of women using archaeological evidence to investigate the concepts of prestige, power, and autonomy. To achieve this goal, Hegmon et al. (2000, 81) looked at two categories of evidence: 1) architecture and the use of space, and 2) the location of gendered labor, household organization, and restrictions on access.

On the basis of the results of these analyses, they argued that there was little evidence of gender differentiation from the early Pithouse period (AD 500) to Post-Classic period (AD 1250); however, there was some evidence that could have been interpreted to show slight social differentiation during the Classic Mimbres period (AD 1000–1130). Furthermore, they found that the homogenous material culture (e.g., the location and deposition of metates and standardized hearth features) recovered from several Mimbres sites indicates that ancestral groups in the Classic period shared a similar ideology—this implies evidence of group or community conformity. However, this does not mean that either men or women had higher status, power, and autonomy. Finally, after the Classic period, Mimbres people preferred to disperse their settlements into the East Mimbres region in addition to reducing the scale of the society from large villages to smaller hamlets. This might indicate that these people would have obtained more individual autonomy (Hegmon et al. 2000).

This example reveals how Mimbres archaeologists have reconstructed agency (i.e., of women) and structure (i.e., of the Mimbres culture) using the practice theory, and it demonstrates how gender study enables us to open up more conversations pertaining to archaeological interpretations of the past.

Agency and Structure Regarding Mimbres Pottery

More recently, many archaeologists (Hegmon and Kulow 2005; Hegmon et al. 2018; LeBlanc 2004) have attempted to reconstruct agency and structure using practice theory to focus on individual Mimbres artists (agency) and the process of innovation in Mimbres pottery designs. By looking at agency in the Mimbres culture, these scholars further attempt to understand the organization of production and the social implications of the design tradition (Hegmon 2008, 220).

LeBlanc (1983, 2004; LeBlanc and Ellis 2001) focused on how individual potters manufactured the Mimbres pottery vessels. On the basis of his stylistic analysis of Mimbres bowl designs, LeBlanc (2004) suggested that there were relatively few specialists who were painting the designs in the Mimbres region, and those artists would have been competing with each other for manufacturing Mimbres vessels during the Classic period.

Hegmon and Kulow (2005) also considered the act of painting a design as a form of agency, and the overall style of that design might represent structure. They analyzed approximately 700 Mimbres bowls dating from the Late Pithouse period to the Classic Mimbres period, and they attempted to tease out the concept of "innovation" by identifying anomalous designs. On the basis of their research, they found that several new designs were present for a short time; these bowl designs were not incorporated into the overall tradition. In contrast, some anomalies were accepted and incorporated into the overall tradition through time. The latter, according to Hegmon and Kulow (2005, 330), could be considered as innovations. The study of anomalous designs and innovations, according to Hegmon and Kulow (2005), allows archaeologists to address the recursive relationship between agency and structure in the Mimbres region.

Hegmon and her colleagues (2018) have also investigated the social significance of meaning(s), and meaningfulness, of the Mimbres pottery designs using their spatial and contextual distributions within the Mimbres River

Valley. They derived their analytical data from data in the Mimbres Pottery Images Digital Database (MimPIDD), and they have focused on group affiliation and demography. The authors conclude that there is no contextual or spatial differentiation between burial practices and related pottery remains. They state, "All the sites have the same suites of designs and motifs. Burials of males and females, and of people of various ages, also have the same suites of designs" (Hegmon et al. 2018).

Their tentative conclusion allows us to conceive that Mimbres people had a high degree of cultural unity and identity (i.e., similar pottery paintings). They also found that the lack of diversity may indicate that different Mimbres Classic painted bowls may have been produced by only a few potters (or agency), and these end products were distributed across the entirety of the Mimbres region. In terms of understanding potential deep meanings of Mimbres iconography, Hegmon and her colleagues' study help us conceptualize the social significance of the designs and motifs, particularly group affiliation and personal identity such as age, gender, and social status.

DIVERSE INTERPRETATIONS OF MIMBRES POTTERY DESIGNS AND MOTIFS

In tandem with the discussion of the development of post-processual archaeology in the Mimbres region, I will also discuss how ethnologists, folklorists, archaeologists, and art historians have described and interpreted the Mimbres black-on-white pottery designs for over one hundred years (e.g., Brody [1977] 2004; Carr 1979; Fewkes 1914, 1923; Hegmon and Trevathan 1996; Moulard and Taylor 1984; Schaafsma 1999; Shafer 1995, 2003; Thompson 1994, 1999). Drawing on the post-processual goal, which is the integration of multiple interpretations, the following paragraphs summarize how many scholars have described and interpreted the designs and motifs of Mimbres pottery. These will help readers to follow and understand the authors' discussions and arguments, particularly in Chapter 5 (i.e., interpretations of Mimbres pottery designs and motifs by five Hopi artists).

Jess Walter Fewkes, an ethnologist, introduced a great number of Mimbres decorated pottery to the general public in the early twentieth century (1916, 1923). In the early 1920s, Fewkes asserted that understanding Native American myths and folklores is crucial for scholars, stating, "If we were familiar with the folklore of the vanished race of the Mimbres, we would be able to interpret these naturalistic pictures or explain their significance in Indian mythology" (1923, 4). In his descriptions and interpretations of Mimbres designs and motifs, Fewkes relied on analogies to Hopi rituals and ceremonial items because the Hopis were thought to be descendants of the Mimbres culture.

Fewkes also compared Mimbres designs and motifs with Sikyatki pottery (prehistoric pottery originally manufactured during the fifteenth and sixteenth centuries) designs in Hopi (1923, 6), as he recognized some similarities and differences between the designs of Sikyatki and Mimbres, stating that former designs represented conventionalized mythic animals, but the Mimbres designs exemplify "realistic ideas" (1923, 18).

In addition to the comparison between Mimbres and Hopi ceramic paintings, Fewkes argued that Mimbres figurative motifs and geometric designs are more similar to ancient ceramics created by Keres than by Tanoan speakers (1923, 7), though he did not explicitly account for his reasoning. Although Fewkes contributed a great deal to the description of Mimbres Classic bowls recovered from Old Town and other sites in the early twentieth century, his interpretations relied heavily on direct "analogy" to Hopi designs and motifs to those on Mimbres pottery. He, however, did not focus his interpretations on testimony of the direct descendants of Hopis, which would be presumably different from Fewkes's interpretations.

In an edited volume titled *Mimbres Pottery: Ancient Art of the American Southwest* (Brody et al. 1983), Tony Berlant and J. J. Brody explored numerous Mimbres pottery designs and motifs and their underlying meanings. Berlant (1983, 20) asserted that the Mimbres aesthetic is similar to the Chinese and Taoist conceptualization of a yin-yang type of sensibility. Berlant (1983, 20) said,

> Each delineation of a form simultaneously defines the form and creates the shape of space around it. Almost invariably, the two elements [black and white color] are so perfectly balanced that figure-ground relationships disappear. There are no negative spaces.

Berlant noticed that background and foreground paintings on Mimbres painted pottery are inseparable, and the painting seems to show that animals and humans have the same spirit, saying "that humanity is part of a cosmic process of transformation and change" (Berlant 1983, 20). On the basis of his perception of Mimbres black-on-white paintings, Berlant also considered key aesthetic concepts, including duality (yin-yang), symmetrical balance, animism, and the relationship between humans and the universe or cosmology.

Brody (1983), an art historian and anthropologist, also attempted to generalize and explore the deep meanings of Mimbres designs and motifs. He investigated basic compositional layouts, various figurative designs (e.g., birds, mammals, insects, fish, and humans), and historical contexts. On the basis of his analysis of more than 7,000 pieces of Mimbres Classic pottery vessels, Brody argued that the makers and users of Mimbres pottery shared a set of rules, concluding that the end products of Mimbres pottery vessels give evidence of similar manufacturing processes and painting techniques. For Brody, the deep meanings of Mimbres pottery designs and motifs cannot be completely understood by archaeologists, art historians, and other scholars. However, he argued that there are myriad ways to interpret potential deep meanings of Mimbres designs and motifs, and he offered several methods.

Brody's investigation of Mimbres Classic paintings revealed that birds and nonhuman mammals occur in approximately 50 percent of the existing designs; human motifs were depicted in about 15 percent; fish-related designs were represented in 10 percent; and insects, amphibians, reptiles, and mythic creatures compose the remaining 25 percent. Brody (1983, 114) found that 1) most Mimbres figurative paintings are a depiction of a single creature; 2) the majority of Mimbres figurative designs are related to food animals; and 3) plant-related motifs are rare. Brody further argues that while it might be difficult to interpret the deep meanings of those paintings (e.g., mammals, birds, insects, and reptiles), anonymous designs and motifs (e.g., compositional or multiple paintings) offer scholars the potential to reconstruct and understand their deep meanings through analogy between Mimbres paintings and mythical and/or folklore stories from oral traditions and ethnographic records. For example, Brody argues that the integration of *Popol Vuh*—the Maya Book of the Dead—would be one method by which we can understand mythical stories depicted on Mimbres Classic vessels.

In addition to the use of the Mayan mythology, Brody asserts that ethnographic information collected in the late nineteenth and twentieth centuries provides possible interpretations of Mimbres paintings. Brody (1983, 110) states,

> The Pueblos of Hopi and Zuni may provide the best clues about the original meanings of Mimbres art. The oral histories and mythologies recorded at those Pueblos late in the nineteenth century form the earliest and most complete set of Pueblo traditions known to outsiders.

It is interesting to note that according to Brody (1983), although Mimbres paintings have fascinated southwesterners for many years, the impact of the use and adaptation of Mimbres designs and motifs on mainstream contemporary art has been minimal, with the exception of adapting Mimbres designs and motifs on contemporary pottery created by San Ildefonso and Acoma potters.

Although Brody emphasizes the importance of integrating Mayan mythologies as a probable source of interpretation of Mimbres designs and motifs, he cautions that the specific iconography of the Mimbres paintings differs dramatically from that of Mesoamerica, stating, "Mimbres paintings were very much a southwestern expression" (1983, 123), suggesting that archaeologists should not rely solely on Mayan mythologies to understand Mimbres motifs (1977, 209–10). Brody also asserts that it is difficult for archaeologists to use the direct historical approach (i.e., the concept that knowledge relating to historical periods is extended back into earlier times) to understand Mimbres pottery designs because the cultural affiliation between the Mimbres people and modern Native American groups has not been clearly demonstrated.

Recently, several scholars have published noteworthy interpretations of Mimbres paintings on ceramics. Gilman and her colleagues (Gilman et al. 2015) explore the connection to Mayan mythology, particularly to the stories of the Hero Twins in the *Popol Vuh* (Tedlock 1985). Gilman et al. argue that some of the representative Mimbres paintings are explicit illustrations of the Hero Twins saga, particularly depictions of the elder and younger brothers, drawings of reincarnated fishmen and fish, seven macaws, sun and deer symbolizing the older twin, and moon and rabbit symbolizing the younger twin (Gilman et al. 2015). Their study of the Mimbres iconography correspondence with the macaw and its Hero Twin saga is persuasive; however, it is important to consider that these Hero Twin depictions on Mimbres Classic pottery were found on only 30 out of the approximately 6,000 bowls in their dataset derived from the MimPIDD (Gilman et al. 2015, 98). This is indeed a small number, but an interesting number of related depictions.

Finally, Berlant and Maurer (2017) offer an alternative hypothesis regarding potential deep meanings of Mimbres iconographic and geometric designs, though their final interpretations are not yet completed. Using the tenets of cognitive archaeology, they argue that Mimbres black-on-white painted ceramic bowls represent abstract ideas of trance-state visual experiences by potters who ingest psychoactive plants, namely datura. They argue that several Mimbres themes were illustrated based on the ingestion of datura, which transports shamans into a trance-like state; thus, some of the motifs depict different stages of the trance state. Their hypothesis is plausible, and I agree with their finding for some designs and motifs. However, it is still difficult to believe that "all" Mimbres potters ingested psychoactive plants of datura prior to painting on pottery.

One criticism of their argument is that several geometric designs on Mimbres vessels are not exactly equivalent to the depiction of datura. For example, the Hopi artists in our project identified a myriad of step designs and interlocking cloud designs, but they found incredibly few flower or datura designs. In addition, when we examine geometric designs on Mimbres pottery, it is possible to see similar geometric designs on bowls and jars created by neighboring groups, such as Ancestral Pueblo and Hohokam. Thus, if we follow Berlant and Maurer's hypothesis, one would postulate that these other groups are all under the influence of datura and experiencing the same effects. Did all Ancestral Pueblo and Hohokam potters go through the same trance-state visual experiences prior to the painting stage? There is not sufficient evidence to support this claim.

Designs from the Ancient Mimbreños with a Hopi Interpretation by Fred Kabotie

Fred Kabotie (1900–1986), a renowned Hopi painter, has contributed a great deal of information related to the interpretation of potential deep meanings of Mimbres designs and motifs. In the early twentieth century, Kabotie was one of only a few Native American artists who recognized the uniqueness of the paintings on Mimbres pottery. In 1939, at the Awatovi excavation in Arizona, Cornelius B. Cosgrove, who excavated Swarts Ruin, introduced Kabotie to literature on Mimbres pottery, exposing him to the unique and intriguing designs and motifs of Mimbres pottery vessels. During Kabotie's fellowship at the Museum of Modern Art in New York, he became more and more interested in the Mimbres pottery designs, particularly in their resemblance to Hopi cultural material (Belknap and Kabotie 1977, 76).

After rereading several Mimbres archaeological reports, Kabotie began to draw designs related to Hopi life. On the basis of his observations, Kabotie states, "I felt that some of the clan symbolism definitely tied in with ours, especially designs showing a relationship between the Water Clan and the Bear Clan" (Belknap and Kabotie 1977, 76). In his interpretations of Mimbres paintings, Kabotie considered key anthropological terms related to clan symbols, katsina motifs, and motifs that may correspond to sorcery, humility, and/or disturbance prior to the depopulation of the Mimbres area (Belknap and Kabotie 1977; Kabotie 1982).

Kabotie admits that his interpretation of Mimbres designs and motifs was derived from his own life experiences and artistry, alluding to individual, personal bias in his interpretation. However, I contend that Kabotie's contribution was compelling in other ways. I believe that integrating Native Americans' interpretations of Mimbres designs and motifs is a crucial component of reconstructing past Mimbres lifeways (see Chapter 5), because as Kabotie states, "While archaeologists and other students are working on the outlines of its history, making it clearer year by year, they cannot completely appreciate the feelings and responses which come instinctively from one who has lived in that culture" (1982, xiv).

CRITIQUES OF POST-PROCESSUAL APPROACH

One of the challenges of critiquing the post-processual paradigm in the Mimbres study area is that it has not been commonly practiced. For example, in Roth and her colleagues' edited collection (Roth et al. 2018), *New Perspectives on Mimbres Archaeology*, in which they updated current scholarship of the Mimbres area by soliciting the research of more than twenty Mimbres archaeologists, only one paper was carried out by agency and structural approach (i.e., Hegmon et al. 2018).

That said, there are still a number of concerns about the limitations of the post-processual framework. First, when looking at Native American artifacts, for example, one of the key questions is whose narratives and voices archaeologists ought to implement for their interpretations. This is a major problem because in the post-processual paradigm, all people's voices and narratives matter for all archaeological interpretations. Then, a simple question arises: "Whose voices and narratives should North Americans listen to? Who has more authority pertaining to interpretations of archaeological records?"

Second, to extend the first point, Madonna Moss pointed out that many North American archaeologists believe that they are doing both scientific and humanistic archaeological research, but they still retain the ultimate authority over archaeological sites and materials. According to Moss (2005, 585),

> For example, even though the National Register guidelines cited above have been updated to include language about "associated values," some archaeologists still operate under the assumption that archaeological sites are eligible to the National Register only for their data potential. Consequently, this type of thinking can lead to statements that some Native Americans as well as some archaeologists might find offensive or anachronistic.

Many North American archaeologists, especially those who conduct their research in the Mimbres region, have not integrated enough multivocality and multiple perspectives, especially of Native Americans (Watkins 2003). It is crucial for North American archaeologists to reconsider how we construct the past because it has relevance to people other than ourselves (i.e., archaeologists). This allows us to more productively and more deeply acknowledge the contributions of those not trained as archaeologists in a Western scientific paradigm (particularly Indigenous people or Native Americans) for archaeological research as well as archaeological interpretations.

In the next chapter, I will discuss how archaeologists have employed multivocality in archaeological research, particularly using the collaborative Mimbres Pottery Workshop as an example of the method.

Chapter 5

Multivocality

Five Hopi artists agreed that the large bird in the center could be a representation of a crane (Figure 2.1). Although there are not many cranes in areas where Hopi live today, these Hopi artists asserted that they have seen cranes near the Hopi reservation. Interestingly, Gwen Setalla mentioned that the potter or the Mimbres people in general would probably have been able to see cranes upon their migration journeys prior to the Hopi's arrival at their homeland. All Hopi artists stressed that the representation of the crane implies an important message of water or a water source. Ramson Lomatewama explicitly stated that birds have connections to water (to rain). That's why the symbol of birds is exceptionally important to the Hopi. Spencer Nutima, Gerald Lomaventema, and Gwen Setalla believe that the crane symbol characterizes the crane clan, which might have become extinct.

MULTIVOCALITY

In response to the post-processual movement, archaeologists were in search of new ways to interpret artifacts. One of the emerging methodologies was the multivocal approach. Since the 1990s, several American archaeologists have conscientiously attempted to find a common ground for archaeological interpretations using both Western science and Native perspectives (Anschuetz 2005, 2006; Anschuetz et al. 2010; Anyon and Ferguson 1995; Anyon et al. 1997; Bernardini et al. 2021; Colwell and Ferguson 2014; Dongoske et al. 1993; Duff et al. 2008; Duwe and Preucel 2019; Ferguson 1995, 1996, 2003, 2004; Ferguson and Colwell-Chanthaphonh 2006; Ferguson et al. 2000; Habu et al. 2008; Kuwanwisiwma and Ferguson 2004; Mills and Ferguson 1998; Swidler et al. 1997).

Among these scholars, Ian Hodder (1991, 1999, 2004), an advocate of the post-processual paradigm, argued that archaeologists have a responsibility to include interpretations of diverse individuals and groups. When they do so, Hodder stated that multiple voices, or multivocality, would open up the work and interest of archaeology to larger groups that included scholars from different disciplines as well as to craftsmen and artists and, importantly, to Native American communities. Bruce Trigger (2008, 190), another prominent advocate for multivocality, contended, "As for multivocality, I believe that the more questions that are asked and the more narratives of the past that are formulated the better." Trigger emphasized that multiple working hypotheses are necessary for archaeologists to gain alternative interpretations of the past. Simply put, the multivocality framework produces more politically mindful interpretations and addresses many of the concerns raised by post-processual archaeologists.

Post-processualism was not the only reason for the rise of multivocality. In fact, from a legal perspective, multivocality was the result of the 1990 Native American Graves Protection and Repatriation Act (NAGPRA), which required North American archaeologists to consult with affiliated and federally recognized Native American groups. After NAGPRA's implementation, there was a large increase in the number of collaborative projects between American archaeologists and Native American groups (e.g., Duwe and Preucel 2019; Ferguson and Colwell-Chanthaphonh 2006). Indigenous archaeologists have worked with North American archaeologists to translate their cultural and archaeological values into heritage management plans that supplant colonial practices. Multivocal collaborations also helped North American archaeologists consider and implement Native Americans' alternative ways of knowing and reconstructing the past.

Since the NAGPRA implementation, the number of Native American and Indigenous archaeologists in the field has also gradually increased, and they have engaged in developing an Indigenous archaeological paradigm and methodology of their own (Atalay 2006). Indigenous archaeology seeks to engage and empower Indigenous people in the preservation of their heritage and to correct perceived inequalities in archaeology today. It also attempts to incorporate non-material elements of cultures, such as oral traditions, into the wider historical narrative. Indigenous archaeology deals with issues previously overlooked by Western-trained archaeologists, such as 1) the repatriation of Indigenous and Native American remains; 2) combating the stereotypes or biases of non-Indigenous archaeologists' Western (more rational and valid than other ways) or imperialistic perspectives toward Indigenous lands, objects, and human remains by employing their own perspectives and practices; and 3) the stewardship and preservation of Indigenous people's cultures and heritage sites. These aspects have encouraged the development of more collaborative relationships between North American archaeologists and Indigenous people, and they have increased the involvement of Indigenous people in archaeology and its related policies.

The relationships between museums and Native Americans have also improved since the establishment of the NAGPRA because it required museum staff to consult tribal peoples regarding human remains and objects curated at museums (Boast and Enote 2014; Colwell-Chanthaphonh 2010; Colwell 2020). Colwell (2020) argues that collaboration is one of the most important tools to decolonize the museums. Full decolonization of museums would mean that Indigenous and Native Americans have true equality in power, authority, and resources pertaining to tangible and intangible remains created and used by their ancestors. However, as Colwell (2020) points out, museums continue to hold the power and authority over these remains. For example, museum staff (e.g., curators as well as coordinators of exhibitions and outreach) generally decide which projects to carry out and whom they ought to invite to an exhibit planning and operation. In other words, it is important to recognize that museum events and activities are designed to serve the museum's goals and purposes.

Museums also control resources, meaning that money and key resources are generally allocated by the museum staff (Colwell 2020). According to Colwell, "Grants, endowments, and other substantial financial resources are often more accessible to museums than communities [Indigenous and Native American]. Then, once funding is secured, grants are controlled and administered by the museums." To overcome the inequality of power, authority, and resources, "post-colonial collaboration" between the museums and Indigenous/Native American communities is crucial (Colwell 2020).

One way to improve the post-colonial collaboration is to include Indigenous and Native American communities' perspectives and voices in correcting descriptions and interpretations of museum objects recorded by ethnographers and historians in the past. By listening to and integrating voices from Native American community members and, importantly, listening to and honoring how Native groups want to interact with the public and their own communities, archaeologists can record ethnographic documentation to help correct biased records of museum collections and help create opportunities for Native peoples to engage with the public and represent their own views. This will make records and exhibits more accurate or less error-filled in American archaeology because many archaeologists in the United States have heavily relied on late nineteenth-century or early twentieth-century ethnographic records as a frame of reference to understand and reconstruct archaeological interpretations. To improve the post-colonial collaboration in archaeology, it is important for American archaeologists to understand how Native people have different ontologies and ways of knowing.

Mimbres Case Studies

When I became a museum director, multivocality became an increasingly important part of my thinking about the interpretation and curation of Native American artifacts. At that time, I also realized that our museum's records were fairly descriptive and limited. For example, the description of the crane-like Mimbres pottery vessel (Figure 2.1) was a one-page document that focused on the size and shape of the vessel and the temporal and spatial information of the bowl. It said nothing about the people who made it, the procuring and processing of materials, and the symbolism of the crane. Archaeologists who excavated the bowl also classified it as "Classic Mimbres" based on the zoomorphic design.

My conundrum at the beginning of museum directorship was how I could include Native American perspectives in the descriptions and interpretations of our collection and exhibitions. Central to this challenge was figuring out how to develop relationships with Native American communities and conduct outreach programs with them. Fortunately, I was introduced to Atsunori Ito, a Japanese anthropologist who had strong connections with Hopi artists, and he helped begin my first multivocal collaboration.

Criticism of Multivocality

While multivocality is an important development in archaeological research, like other methodologies, it has limitations. First, multivocal research works well when carried out in areas where recognized descendant communities are still living nearby. However, when conducting multivocal in areas, such as the Mimbres cultural area, where descendant communities (e.g., federally recognized Pueblo groups) do not live in the area, archaeologists can have a difficult time finding descendants with whom to conduct the multivocal approach. Second, when archaeologists use the multivocal approach, the end product of their research seems to present either only Native Americans' perspectives or only scientific perspectives. In other words, there is not a unified product of both scientific and humanistic perspectives. Although there are several limitations in multivocality, what follows is an account and impression of our effort to interpret Mimbres pottery. This case study demonstrates how the multivocal approach can resolve some of these limitations discussed in this section.

CASE STUDY DESIGN

As I discussed in Chapter 1, the Mimbres Pottery Design Workshop, which was directed by a Japanese cultural anthropologist, Dr. Atsunori Ito (Principal

Table 5.1. Each artist's background information.

Artist Name	Clan Affiliation	Village	Craft Expertise
Ramson Lomatewama	Eagle	Hotevilla	Katsina dolls and blown glass
Gerald Lomaventema	Bear	Shongopavi	Silversmith (jewelry)
Gwen Setalla	Bear	Maternal: Mishongnovi Paternal: Sichomovi Born and raised in Kearns Canyon	Pottery
Spencer Nutima	Greasewood	Oraibi	Katsina dolls and silversmith (jewelry)
Ed Kabotie	Badger	Shongopavi/ Santa Clara	Painting, song, silversmith (jewelry), katsina dolls

Investigator), included five Hopi artists: Ramson Lomatewama, Gerald Lomaventema, Gwen Setalla, Spencer Nutima, and Ed Kabotie (Table 5.1). We conducted this workshop as a singular case study for using a multivocal approach in collaboration with the source community.

In the following sections, I will discuss 1) how we selected the Mimbres pottery vessels we decided to interpret; 2) how and why we visited the Mimbres study area; 3) how we recorded the descriptions and interpretations of these Hopi artists' voices; and 4) what and how we disseminated the results of this collaborative work, which included an exhibition of new art inspired by the Hopi artists' experiences during the project. Then, I will review how each Hopi artist described and interpreted five zoomorphic and anthropomorphic bowls out of thirty-seven total vessels.

It is important to note that since the descriptions and interpretations of the rest of the twelve anthropomorphic and zoomorphic bowls and sixteen geometric bowls and jars are in depth and long, I do not include them in this book. I also do not include one corrugated vessel and two plain wares because these do not show any painted designs. However, readers will be able to read those descriptions after Ito finalizes entry of all thirty-seven pottery vessels into the Info-Forum Museum Project database at the National Museum of Ethnology (Minpaku) in Japan in the future.

In the last section of this chapter, I will share my observations of and reflections on reviewing Mimbres pottery designs and motifs with the Hopi artists. While we were recording these Hopi artists' narratives regarding numerous Mimbres pottery designs and motifs, I wrote down my own observations and impressions about how the Hopi artists reflected and responded to their views and thoughts regarding ancient arts and potters.

Selecting and Reviewing Mimbres Pottery

We initially selected all twelve pieces of Mimbres pots and utilitarian vessels curated at the University Museum at New Mexico State University (NMSU). However, since NMSU's collection only consisted of four figurative Mimbres pottery vessels, we decided to include twenty-two additional Mimbres pottery vessels curated at Geronimo Springs Museum (nonprofit) in Truth or Consequences, New Mexico. While selecting these vessels, we focused on diverse depictions of potential fish, reptile, mammal, and andromorphic designs and motifs as well as varied geometric designs, such as spiral, rectangular, and diagonal lines.

The Mimbres vessels curated at both the NMSU museum and Geronimo Springs Museum unfortunately did not have provenience or context information; the majority were donated by local residents in the Mimbres region. Under this circumstance, when selecting these pieces, we attempted to avoid choosing Mimbres vessels showing evidence of a "kill hole," which is an intentional puncture at the distinct circular hole(s) located in the center of the bowls. A bowl with a kill hole presumably indicates that the bowl was used as part of a ritual and sacred burial practice. It is a common belief that kill holes served as a conduit from a living world to a spiritual world. To resolve the lack of provenience information and the issue of cultural sensitivity regarding Mimbres painted vessels with the Hopi reviewers, we selected Mimbres pottery vessels without a kill hole. However, when we recognized a potential hole on the side (not center) of a Mimbres bowl, we used a TV monitor to show the photograph of the bowl to the Hopi artists to see if they were comfortable enough to review it.

Finally, one Mimbres bowl was eliminated from further discussions in this book due to a depiction of a culturally and personally sensitive motif inside the bowl. Therefore, a total of thirty-three Mimbres pottery vessels were reviewed by the Hopi artists, and of these, I will discuss five zoomorphic and anthropomorphic Mimbres bowls in this chapter.

Visiting the Mimbres Valley and Upper Gila Regions

In addition to recording the Hopi artists' reviews of the Mimbres pottery designs, we carried out a field trip to the Mimbres region for two days. Since the Hopi artists live in the northeastern portion of Arizona, the purpose of the field trip was to familiarize the artists with the environment, topography, prehistory, and history of the Mimbres culture area. Therefore, we contend that part of this project is to reconnect Hopi artists with those aspects of their history at the center of this study. This allowed the artists to experience the same landscapes as their ancestor groups, which facilitated unraveling potential meanings of Mimbres pottery designs and motifs.

To achieve this goal, we visited the heartland of the Mimbres Valley and Upper Gila areas in the Mimbres region with those Hopi artists after completing the initial review of the Mimbres pottery at NMSU (Figure 5.1). Since the time was limited and some areas needed a special visiting permit to access, we decided to visit the Mimbres Cultural Heritage Site, which included a site tour of Mattock Ruin dating to the Pithouse and Classic Mimbres periods. We also visited another Pithouse and Mimbres site (TJ Ruin), the Gila Cliff Dwellings National Monument, and other areas along the Mimbres River. Ideally, we would have liked to visit the Mimbres sites where our reviewed pottery vessels were discovered, but since many vessels did not have any provenience information, we decided to visit these representative Mimbres sites and surrounding areas in the Mimbres region.

By visiting the landscape and archaeological sites, the Hopi artists were able to experience the area for themselves, allowing them to delve into the environment and try to identify with Mimbres potters' perspectives and aesthetics. In addition, since Gwen Setalla wanted to procure local clay and temper for manufacturing her exhibition items, we tested and collected some useful clay and temper during the field trip.

Figure 5.1. A Gila Cliff Dwellings personnel describing the landscape of one of the Mimbres sites to the five Hopi artists.

Recording Narrative Data

After we recorded the Hopi artists' narratives regarding the Mimbres pottery designs and motifs, we processed them by following Ito's Info-Forum Museum reviewing methods (Ito et al. 2021; Ito et al. 2020; Ito 2016, 2017, 2019, 2020). Using this method, we first recorded the artists' narratives during their examination of each piece of pottery by a video. Then, these recorded narratives were transcribed into a Word document. Consequently, Ito ensured the transcribed words in English and Hopi were accurate, and he also could eliminate words and phrases that were culturally sensitive or personal. Finally, the end product of the recorded narratives consisted of written documents (memos and drawings), recorded films, and photos which were curated at the National Museum of Ethnology (Minpaku) in Japan. These materials will be available online on the Minpaku's Info-Forum Museum Project database in the future.[1]

Producing Their Own Artistries and Exhibition

Another part of this project related to a request that each artist produce new and innovative artistic items based on their experience and inspiration from the trip to the Mimbres region and from the project as a whole.[2] The participating Hopi artists produced new artistic items based on their expertise, including pottery (by Gwen Setalla), blown glass objects (by Ramson Lomatewama), silver jewelry (by Gerald Lomaventema), paintings (by Ed Kabotie), and katsina dolls (by Spencer Nutima).

Importantly, Ito and I initially proposed to showcase the exhibition at a gallery of the NMSU University Museum from May 2018 to April 2019 after Ito went through the process of dealing with culturally sensitive matters regarding the artists' personal, lineage, clan, and/or the Hopi as a whole. However, we needed to alter our plan because of culturally and personally sensitive matters raised by the Hopi artists pertaining to the curation of NAGPRA-related human remains and funerary objects inside the museum.

In the preliminary conversations with the Hopi artists, Ito and I noted that the museum has curated NAGPRA-related human remains and funerary objects. On the basis of the information, several Hopi artists expressed their concern that they were not comfortable displaying their artistries near these human remains and funerary objects. One Hopi reviewer asserted that a negative spirit would harm their artistries if we used the space close to their ancestors physically and spiritually. Because of this, Ito and I decided to propose an alternative place. The American Indian Student Center generously offered us their gallery space for our exhibition, and the collaborators (the Hopi artists, Ito, and I) accepted their invitation (Figure 5.2).

Figure 5.2. The five Hopi artists, the author (left), Gerald Lomaventema, Spencer Nutima, Ed Kabotie, Gwen Setalla, Ramson Lomatewama, and Atsunori Ito (right) at the American Indian Student Center on April 26, 2019.

Importantly, because the Hopi artists had brought this concern to my attention, I recognized that the presence of human remains presented long-term problems for the viability of the museum as a place of collaboration moving forward. As the museum director, I decided to relocate the remains immediately. One major reason is that the museum hosts the American Indian Week every spring, and many Native American groups use the building for the preparation of their performances. I was afraid that if these groups became aware that the museum possesses human remains and funerary objects inside the building, they would not feel respected and that this might subvert my goals to make the museum a more collaborative place. Because of this matter, after this workshop was completed in 2019, the museum staff transferred all NAGPRA materials to another location, where they are currently being stored with respect to Native American feelings and beliefs. More recently, in 2021 the museum staff initiated a NAGPRA consultation with ten Native American tribal groups in order to begin to the repatriation process.

The aim of the exhibition was to showcase collaborative work among the Hopi artists who have participated in the project and the museum personnel at NMSU, Minpaku, and the Museum of Northern Arizona. Dr. Kelley Hays-Gilpin and museum personnel at the Museum of Northern Arizona facilitated this project regarding the research permit process with the Hopi Cultural Preservation Office and provided Ito and me with advice regarding the collaboration with Hopi artists. The exhibit featured the perspectives and art of the Hopi artists displayed in a space they helped design. When the exhibit opened, the artists were there to participate in a panel discussion and docent-led tours. They also helped us address how we could engage in community outreach related to available information in the Info-Forum Museum Project. In the exhibition, we integrated recorded voices, photos, written documents, and films as well as innovative artistries produced by the Hopi artists.

Workshop at the NMSU University Museum, NMSU Art Museum, and Branigan Cultural Center

To disseminate the results of the Mimbres Pottery Workshop,[3] I coordinated a workshop at the NMSU University Museum, NMSU Art Museum, and Branigan Cultural Center in Las Cruces, New Mexico, from October 24 to 28, 2019. The original idea of the workshop was proposed by the Hopi reviewers when the University Museum staff asked a simple question: "What else do you want to do regarding the results of this workshop?" The Hopi artists requested to do a workshop in Las Cruces; this allowed NMSU students as well as local community members to learn about the history of the Hopi arts and its aesthetics and culture.

Three Hopi artists participated in this workshop, and each artist engaged in three activities: 1) giving a lecture; 2) demonstrating their manufacturing process; and 3) offering a show-and-tell of their artistries. Gerald Lomaventema gave a talk about the history of Hopi silversmiths and demonstrated tufa casting; Gwen Setalla gave a lecture about the history of her Hopi pottery craftmanship and the difference between traditional and non-traditional pottery making; and Ramson Lomatewama came to the Introduction to Native American Studies class, where he discussed Native American perspectives and worldviews, and demonstrated the process of making of blown glass art to the public.

After finishing lectures and demonstrations, these Hopi artists did a show-and-tell of their products at the Branigan Cultural Center in Las Cruces. More than fifty people visited our booth and asked about the manufacturing processes of Hopi pottery, blown glass, and silver jewelry and the meaning behind these objects. Overall, the workshop was a success, and the Hopi artists wanted to come back and carry out a similar workshop in the future.

DESCRIPTIONS AND INTERPRETATIONS OF MIMBRES POTTERY FIGURATIVE DESIGNS AND MOTIFS

The data we collected from this multivocal study consists of the Hopi artists' discussions of the pottery designs and motifs (in which they shared ideas and interpretations with one another and us) and the individual narratives which were collected for the curation of the exhibition of their work at the NMSU

American Indian Student Center (these consists of reflections on the Mimbres pottery that inspired their work, insights to their artwork, and thoughts on their experience in the study). The complete discussions on Mimbres pottery designs and motifs will be published by Ito at Minpaku in the future. In the following sections, focusing on one pot and artist at a time, I summarize portions of the Hopi artists' discussions and selected portions of the individual narratives from the exhibition.

Ramson Lomatewama's Description and Interpretation of the Mimbres Bowl G476-4

The double fish design was the pot that inspired Ramson's work for the exhibition. Below is Ramson's interpretation of the pot, followed by a discussion of his artwork that draws on the Mimbres design and a reflection on the Mimbres Valley field trip.

This is interesting to me because it does have two fish instead of just one in it. I haven't seen this before. But I'm sure there are probably more pots out there that also have two fish or maybe even more than that. I was really . . . I'm really intrigued by Gwen's idea of maybe these being hallmarks of sorts for different potters. To me, things like that are worth looking into. Maybe

Figure 5.3.

Figure 5.4.

they were, maybe they weren't. But just to at least pursue that question I think is really important. Just maybe someone could do a dissertation on just the rings and nothing else. But that I . . . when she mentioned that I would . . . that really just got me to think about the way we identify our own pieces. Today it's primarily our initials or our clan symbols. But maybe the people who made these pots, maybe this was their way of kind of signing their pieces, you might say. And the other thing that I got me to thinking was Gerald's question about the use of these pots. Because we do use baskets and pottery as exchanges during weddings. Today we use quilts for naming ceremonies. And did they have that same practice, were these gift exchanges. Maybe somebody's *möwii* brought this bowl over, with food in it. And . . . but we don't know about the social structure back then. There's really no evidence of marriage or anything like that to help us to answer that. So, these are just things that we asked without really. Maybe we shouldn't expect to find an answer. But there's still interesting questions. When I was looking at this, it's not the cleanest bowl in terms of the line definitions or the steadiness of the lines. But it was interesting this one in particular to me because I tended to see on the upper part of the bodies the parallel lines and then the wide space and then more parallel lines. And what that made me think of us if I look at a fish in a pond, you see the reflections of the ripples of the water on the backs of the fish. And then underneath it's in the shadow. So, it appears darker. We can actually see the scales. So that was something that I just was looking at. It's really interesting to incorporate lines and checkerboards in there which I don't think the other depiction of fish had. They were pretty much all simpler, not as elaborated as this one. So, I though this one was a pretty interesting piece of pottery, just based on the way it was painted and different segments of the checkerboard and parallel lines. And what I didn't also notice is, this seems to be a purposeful division between the head and the gills and the rest of the body. I think all of them have some kind of separation between the head and the rest of the body of the fish. So those are just my questions. (Arakawa and Ito 2019)

Narrative of His Inspired Product (Figure 5.5)

[I]t was an honor and a privilege to work with you and Mimbres Pottery Project, and when we were asked to create a piece of art that spoke to the history of the Mimbres culture and our own perspectives of it, I decided to draw a connection between the concept of the corn and Hopi culture. So, the corn maiden is representative of the feminine principle in Hopi culture. It is also a representative of the connection between the female and the idea of corn being that they're both from the feminine principle and that corn and the female in Hopi culture are the progenitors of life. So, that was that part of it, and then the other part was reflecting back on the history of Hopi culture, because I've always personally believed that the Mimbres people worked into the migrations of the Hopi people, you know, centuries ago, and I was very drawn to the Mimbres culture and the pottery back in the 1990s; it was when I really took an interest in it. And I wanted to combine the idea of the history of the Mimbres culture and the imagery that they used back then, and meld it with the idea of the contemporary times and the Hopi people today. So, you notice that there is an image of a fish, which is reminiscent of the Mimbres image of a fish. There are also tadpoles on the body, as I recall, and the tadpole is life in development, and so I wanted to communicate the progression of life as, as it happens—in the womb through birth, and the cycle of life in general, so those were the major themes that I tried to incorporate into that glass piece. (personal communication, October 27, 2021)

Narrative and Reflection Based on His Experience and Feelings during the Mimbres Valley Field Trip

My name is Ramson Lomatewama. I'm a member of the Hopi tribe from the Third Mesa area on the Hopi Reservation back in Arizona. I've been given a very, very wonderful opportunity to re-experience and experience from

Figure 5.5.

myself the landscape and the history of the Mimbres culture. I've always had a deep interest in Mimbres culture because I see this particular group of people as being a part of my cultural and my personal history. Looking at the pottery and imagining what was going on through the minds of these people as they created this ceramic, gave me insights as to myself and why I've chosen to pursue the things that I have pursued for years. Being here in the Mimbres Valley has given me a chance to walk in history. The one thing that

I feel is that just by coming here I'm part of the history of this area. I imagine the daily life, the struggles, the thoughts that were occurring a thousand years ago. And I often ask myself, were these people thinking the same thoughts as I am now? How were their experiences different? Well, this is 2017 and obviously I cannot really go back there in terms of my physical being but my spiritual being. And the sense of the history and connection to this area and these people remains and it's constant and it's very, very strong. So being inspired by the environment, the leaves falling from the trees, the breeze in the air, the sound of the water rippling down the creeks, the stones that made up the walls of their homes inspires me to experiment with new forms. As a contemporary Hopi artist, glassblowing has been a large part of my life. And a way for me to connect to the history of the people who lived in this area, is something that I would love to continue to explore through the art. I'm a contemporary artist who works in the area of hot glass. And by looking at the pottery, I've been inspired to do creations in the Mimbres tradition from centuries ago. I've taken the environment of today. And I'd like to find ways to integrate the plants and the landscape into the work that I choose to do. And because we are in a much, much more different time and I have worked with sterling silver, I like to combine the sterling silver that I work with, the landscape in forms of rocks and tree branches and a variety of other things from the landscape. And bringing those together with stained glass and hand blown glass will tie in myself, the history, and today's life. So, these are some of the things that I have really come to appreciate and respect even more. This experience here has inspired me to try new things, to try and express myself in terms of my history, my culture, the present and the future. It's with these things in mind that I hope that our posterity, my great-great-great grandchildren will see as a way to try and continue to appreciate and live life to its fullest, to appreciate your history, to appreciate who you are living in the world today, and to envision a world of beauty, a world of happiness, and a world of prosperity for generations to come. (Arakawa and Ito 2019)

Gerald Lomaventema's Description and Interpretation of the Mimbres Bowl 1980.17.476 (Figure 2.1)

The crane-like design was the pottery vessel that inspired Gerald's work for the exhibition. Gerald said,

First thing I noticed that this one looks like it's all intact. The other one has a crack right almost through midway. *Ya ii hinmaatsiwngwu? Atoku, atokuku.* Yeah, that's what we call it. I've seen that in the little . . . especially monsoon season. And there was a clan that was called that also. But I'm not too sure they're still around. It's . . . to me it represents a water source. And I bet as we believe today in Hopi that these are water bird along with the duck. I don't

Figure 5.6.

know how to say this one bird only in Hopi, *patzro*. But this design here is . . . it looks very basic. But it has probably a lot of meaning associated with the rain which I think are represented in the body with the . . . that's some sort of a symbol for that water. But . . . and the three lines is different too. It's different than . . . I don't know what that represents because maybe it's just an expression or a border around the whole design. But still like Gwen mentioned, she has more knowledge about painting. And it would probably be very difficult to go into that bowl and paint that design there. So, I've done a little painting but I'm not very good at it. So, I'm . . . very . . . there's a lot of admiration for these designs because I could see them in silver already just by looking at them. That's probably it. (Arakawa and Ito 2019)

Narrative of His Inspired Product

Hello, my name is Lomaventema. My first name is Gerald and my Hopi name is Lomaventema. This here is a bolo tie of the revival technique of Hopi silversmithing done in the 1930s using coin silver. And the Mimbres inspired design of the water bird in our language is called *atokuku*. So, the

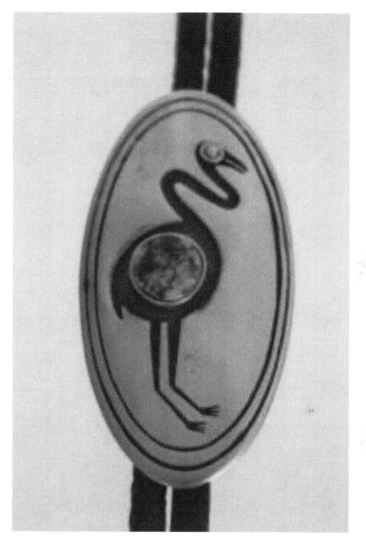

Figure 5.7.

stone is also natural from Bisbee, Arizona, which is rare. And I believe that the Mimbres and the Hopi have a connection just by looking at their design on their pottery. And we'd like to feel a closeness between the two cultures. So very inspiring to see the designs of the pottery of the Mimbres in our jewelry. (Arakawa and Ito 2019)

Narrative and Reflection Based on His Experience and Feelings during the Mimbres Valley Field Trip

This trip and . . . to the Las Cruces and Mimbres Valley. I think it helps an artist to realize that it's not just about trying to make the money, but you have to get inspiration at some point where it becomes not about the money but about creating pieces that have very almost spiritual meaning. So, when I paid . . . when I visited these places, I've gotten a newer sense of where my . . . in a direction I wanted my jewelry to go, which is back to the basics. This is not the only trip that I've taken in the past, but I've visited places like Peru, middle . . . the Middle America, that central of Mexico. And all those places it's all, it mystifies me. And those who are places of our origin, of our ancestors. So being able to come to these places and reconnect with our ancestors in their dwellings and the pottery, gives new inspiration for me. And I hope to create jewelry with these new ideas but using old techniques. I'm trying to get basic as I can as when the silver work was being done in the late 1800s into the early 1900s, the Hopi style of jewelry making. So, I appreciate these visits here and appreciate the museum and Dr. Atsunori and Dr. Fumi. So, *Kwakway.* (Arakawa and Ito 2019)

Figure 5.8.

Figure 5.9.

Gwen Setalla's Description and Interpretation of the Mimbres Bowl G412/13–70 (Figure 5.8)

The hummingbird-like design was the pot that inspired Gwen's work for the exhibition. Gwen said,

Okay this is item number G412/13–70. And I must say before I saw the description of this particular pot, my immediate thoughts were hummingbird. This to me is a depiction of a hummingbird in flight. And the way I come to that conclusion is by the way the wings are painted. They're not painted with straight lines. They are painted with diamond-shaped images indicating that it's fluttering. As well as the tail where it has the three lines in the center with the spaces in between. That to me indicates some kind of movement. So, this would indicate to me a hummingbird that's in flight. As potters we use straight lines, wiggles and whatnot to express certain things, flight, movement, any kind of movement we show with applications of various lines in various forms applying it differently. Again, this one does have a rounded bottom. It does have temper. It looks to have been applied with a white slip-on interior-exterior. Although the exterior has been worn off. You can see much of the fire clouds and very orange, more orange. So, I'm presuming this was at a little higher temperature. It does show signs of damage, cracks, restoration, shows where tape had been used to hold it together. The pigment on there is red paint. Again, on the mouth of the piece as well as lines just below the mouth on the interior rim. And along with that extending from the very last thin line. You can see the . . . looks like diamond shapes. But the way they are applied kind of makes it look as it's got curves to it. I can tell that they probably did the diamond shapes first and then went and did . . . tried to make the straight line on top of that. Because I can see it in the painting where the line overlaps the diamond shapes. Again, very well centered. It does still have some yellow coloration to some of the interior which may have been caused by water damage. And the last line would be interpreted as a potter, from me, as water, which would be this part here. But then that can also be an indication of a flower, different petals of a flower there. This represents it being in flight here as well as this, as the hummingbird flutters. It goes very, very fast. So that could indicate it's been fluttering around. I really love the design on here. I have a . . . I guess you can say, I have a spiritual connection with hummingbirds. And it only just recently came upon me. When I was at work, when I went to work one morning, I was the only one working that day and wasn't very busy. I hadn't eaten breakfast so I took a small breakfast snack along with me. I did my opening routine. And then I decided to step outside in have my breakfast. And we do have a lot of brush located outside the Visitor Center of Homolovi. And one of those attracts a lot of the hummingbirds. It's called the Apache plume. It does have like a pink purple flower on there, dragonflies and a lot of the hummingbirds are attracted to that. So, I sat there and I was just thinking, pondering on different things. Mainly I like to think about the good times that I've had with my parents. And I miss those days. So, I was sitting there thinking about things. And there's this hummingbird. It was purple and blue. And it just flew. And I was sitting there looking. And it came right in front of me like this. And we were looking eye-to-eye. And it was going like this to me. And I was talking to it. And it wouldn't fly away. It just was fluttering there. And I'm like, "Oh, hello have you brought me a message or something?" And we were just looking. And it wasn't scared at all. And so immediately I thought spiritual connection. And it must have fluttered for probably I'd say about 30 seconds or more. And then it started to fly off. But then it went to the left of my shoulder. And it was like they're talking to me which I kind of was looking at the corner of my eye not wanting to startle it and turn around like this. And it looked like it was going to land on my shoulder. And then it went around me. And then it did the same thing here. And then it came back and it started staring at me again. And I was just thinking, "What are you trying to tell me?" And then I sat there and it just kind of flew off and of course the brush was just located right behind me. And it went there and it sat right on the flower. And it didn't . . . it wasn't afraid of me. So, I turned around to look like that and it was still there. And I got up and they kind of started fluttering. But it didn't fly off. And then so . . . after a while I watched it and then I kind of walked away and then it flew off. But then it came back like, "Wait, I forgot to tell you something." So, it flew back to me again. It was flying around me. And it's really, really strange. Because I immediately I felt that spiritual connection or a connection of a message. And it's funny because like a day or two after that, was when Gerald and Ito contacted me, contacted me with regarding this workshop. And this Mimbres workshop is something I've always wanted to do. I've always wanted to learn about the Mimbres pottery. And it was . . . it was to me like, "Yeah, maybe that was the message." And so, I went home and when I told my husband about it, he says, well, he says that in our culture those mean travel. You are going to go somewhere, he says. And then pretty soon all this started coming together. And I immediately thought back to the hummingbird. So now I have a new spirit . . . spiritual respect for the hummingbird. I've always loved hummingbirds. And dragonflies I feel the same way. A lot of depiction on ancestral Hopi pottery of dragonflies. And the dragonflies back then with the Hopi pottery indicated moisture. Because when our Hopi people were on migration, wherever they saw water, where they ever presumed there was a water source nearby, there was always dragonflies around. So that's how they knew that there was water there. So, a lot of the ancestral potters depicted dragonflies on their pottery. So now I have a new love for hummingbirds. And the painting is done very well except for again the lines are not . . . not too straight except for some of it. And the design is . . . to me it's perfect. It's round, the head is round. It's got a nice circular shoulder. Again, the way it's painted indicates that it's in flight. Again, there is some damage to it. So very, very beautiful pot. This is probably my favorite only because of the newfound connection with the hummingbird. I love this one. (Arakawa and Ito 2019)

Narrative of Her Inspired Product

Hi, my name is Gwen Setalla. My matrilineal clan is bear and my father's clan is water. This one here would be considered a fruit bowl. You can put fruit or food in it. The design depicted on the interior is a hummingbird. The hummingbird was very special to me prior to the visit of the Mimbres Valley and studying the pottery, I had an encounter with a hummingbird. I went to work one morning and I was just sitting outside trying to ponder upon some of the things that had happened. And trying to figure things out. And there came this hummingbird. And it just flew right in front of me. And it was like right here in front of me just staring at me. And I looked in the eyes. And we were looking in each other's eyes. And I was like, "oh, hello what are you doing here?" And it just fluttered there for the longest time. Then it went to my left side. And then it went around my head to the other side on my shoulder. And then it fluttered it there for a little bit. And then it flew off. So, to me

Figure 5.10.

that was a blessing of some sort. And I'll always remember that. And when I saw this hummingbird design on the Mimbres pottery, I knew right away that there was going to be some connection with that. There are also designs of clouds and the water wave here. We do also see dragonflies. The dragonflies when I asked an elder what the dragonflies meant depicted on ancestral pottery, he said that the dragonflies represented the migration. When our people were migrating, wherever they saw dragonflies, they knew that a water source was nearby. So therefore, that is where they would stay and live for a little bit. So, I feel that the Mimbres are part of that migration trail and a part of that migration path. So, this one depicts their design as well as the dragonfly design in representation to the migration. (Arakawa and Ito 2019)

Narrative and Reflection Based on Her Experience and Feelings during the Mimbres Valley Field Trip

My name is Gwen Setalla. I am Hopi potter. My matrilineal clan is bear. My patrilineal is water. And I was invited to take part in the Mimbres project or workshop. I really enjoyed it. Our first few days were viewing some of the collections at the University Museum. We did have a lot of fun. We viewed many, many bowls. Majority of those bowls had animal or a bird-like figures. All painted on the inside with broad lining on the outside. Majority of them were black and white with the rims having black paint around the mouth. We did find one or viewed one that had a design on the outside. Kind of looking like interlocking water waves. And I kind of questioned as to whether the Mimbres people had any connection with the people from Chaco Canyon because their designs were very, very quite similar except for the animal and bird figures. We did take a tour of the Mattocks Museum. And there again, we were able to kind of see the lifestyle or how they lived, the Mimbres how they lived. We were able to see many of their dwellings. Much of it had been excavated and covered over. But there was a river flowing nearby. And you could probably see that in the background. It's very, very beautiful, very green. Lots of wildlife, lots of birds. We encountered deer, javelin, turkeys, some lizards I had never seen before. And today we took a trip to the Gila Cliff Dwellings. Very, very beautiful. I had never been through there. We had to cross over several bridges. There's the river that runs through or by the cliff dwellings. When inside climbed the cliff dwellings. And it's just spectacular being up high and looking down into the valley, being able to see the water, the walls across from the cliff dwellings. And we also went to TJ Ranch Ruins site. And there wasn't very much to see there except for a lot of broken potsherds there. And again, a lot that had Mimbres designs on there. Much of the color again was black on white. We did see some what they referred to as San Francisco redware. I believe that I might be coming back here in the future only because it's very beautiful, it's very interesting, fishing, camping, so much to see here. It's a very, very enjoyable if you come from the desert then you come here it's just a really nice place to be. It's like being in the whole new world. So, I really enjoyed it and I'm really glad that I had the opportunity to partake in this workshop. And I hope to learn more about the Mimbres and as far as my works in progress or what I decide, I'm going to make from inspiration of what I seen here I haven't decided yet. So, we'll have to see what that turns out to be. *Askwali.* (Arakawa and Ito 2019)

Ed Kabotie's Description and Interpretation of the Mimbres Bowl 2006.11.05.

The coyote-like design was the pottery vessel that inspired Ed's work for the exhibition. Ed said,

[O]ne of the things I like about this particular piece is the, in the picture that we have here, the one where you can see it from the bottom, it looks like you can really see like the artist . . . their anatomy, their fingers on the piece.

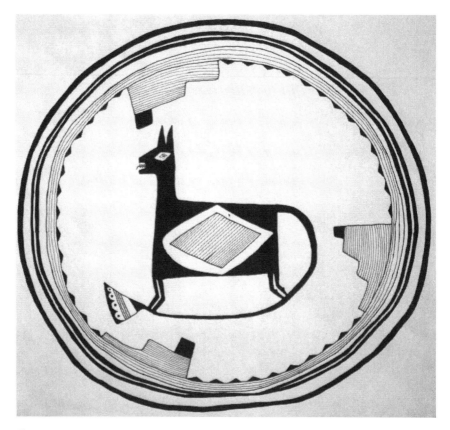

Figure 5.11.

So, I'm really enjoying the interaction between everybody. Because Ramson encourages us not to put our own spin on it, our own experience. But to me it's really hard not to do that with this one. Just because to me he really looks like a coyote. And to me that's the first impression that I get. It looks to me again like there's clouds. And I like to see the black, the stronger moisture. I'm curious if we could just look at the close-up of the bands. Because I'd kind of like to count. And I'm counting spaces not . . . sometimes I'm counting lines but sometimes I'm counting spaces too. And this one has four spaces, it has . . . four spaces here, white spaces in between the lines which could be significant. But it also, to me I guess I like to look at it as a coyote. I'm not . . . I have a real, a personal thing with coyotes. And it's more because not . . . that's not my clan. I'm a badger clan but it was my nickname in Tewa. Because they call you *dee-ee* which means little coyote if . . . when you're mixed blood. And so, it was kind of like a term of endearment but it was kind of like a put-down at the same time so. And I feel like it was something that

Figure 5.12.

for me I had to embrace that nickname at some point to my own self-accep-
tance. The image does too look to me . . . it's . . . this here in Tewa so coyote
is *dee*. But a fox: *po'povi-dee*. So *po'povi* is actually that would literally
translate pumpkin blossom coyote is a fox. And because of their tail, because
it's . . . because of the tail of the fox so this one had kind of to me looks like
he also has something there. It also kind of reminds me of a story as well, of a
coyote story when he was kind of in competition with the snake. And they had
an exchange of hospitality. But the snake when coyote went to snake's home,
snake really . . . when he came or when snake came to visit him, he really
took up coyote's home. So, snake was kind of upset about that or a coyote
was upset about that. So, when he went to visit the snake, then he added to the
tail. And then when he left his tail, he wasn't careful. And so, it got too near
the fire there. And it kind of caught on fire. And then when he went home it
was . . . the fire was chasing him. So, it kind of reminds me of that too. But of
course, those are putting things into it. But those are just things that the image
does for me personally. And I guess I really, I like to think it's a coyote. But
the band around I just wanted to see that too. It's double banded. And then I
just wanted to see the close-up maybe something here. Again, to me like the
Mimbres have a really powerful way of presenting an animal. I feel like in
kind of . . . in maybe the greater culture tends to make everything not alive

that's not human. Things are kind of de-personalized, devalued. We can separate ourselves. We're human beings and then there's all these other life forms that we don't always need to respect if they get in our way. And I feel like the Mimbres have a really powerful way of demonstrating the essence of an animal. The spirit of an animal, the . . . what happens when you see a coyote or when you see a deer. I mean and the feeling that you feel connected with it in your heart. And again, I feel like that's something that's really unique maybe in Native art as opposed to European art. Where a European is trying to draw exactly what he sees. Where to me like this type of traditional work it's what we see but it's also what we feel, how we react to it maybe. And I just . . . I admire the artist. I wonder sometimes how many of these pieces are done by the same person that we look at. Because we have notable potters in our communities. And I think about that how many of these are going to have those type of similarities. But anyway. *Kwakway.* (Arakawa and Ito 2019)

Narrative of His Inspired Product

My name is Ed Kabotie. And this piece is entitled *True American*. And it's a piece that is giving tribute to, what I consider the first documented war for religious freedom in what we call the United States today. We're all very

Figure 5.13.

familiar with July 4th being referred to as Independence Day from the year 1776. However, 100 years before the American Revolution, the Pueblo tribes of northern New Mexico and northern Arizona, warred with Spain in, again what I considered to be the first documented war for religious freedoms in the United States. And we are the only group of Native American people and all of written history to oust an establish European colony from our homeland. So, there are seven stripes in this flag which represent the seven Pueblos language groups: the Tiwa, the Tewa, the Towa, Keres, Zuni, Hopi, and then the Piro which are actually non-existent today. This, here this blue area is showing the land that we fought for the lands of the Colorado Plateau here in its center place, here. And then also the mountains of Navajo Mountain, the San Francisco Peaks, Mt. Taylor, and then Mt. Hesperus in Colorado. So, this is showing, giving tribute to that war. I have coyote here, kind of sticking out his tongue. Because he's been a little bit cynical about the way that we interpret history. He's the one that's been here the whole time. So, he really knows the truth. So, this is *True American.* (Arakawa and Ito 2019)

Narrative and Reflection Based on His Experience and Feelings during the Mimbres Valley Field Trip

Well, let me just start off just by saying thank you to everybody. Yeah, thank you to Fumi, Mirei, and Atsunori. Thank you, Chris [Adams] for all of your help guiding us around. I appreciate everybody's insights. Thank you, Spencer, Ramson, Gerald, and Gwen. Thank you, guys. This is really enriching experience for me. I've always been interested in Mimbres design. I guess when I say always, I'm not sure when that fascination started. I've seen, I guess, what I've probably been most intrigued by is the animals, the way that they express animals. And I've said before that I feel like they have a way of expressing the spirit of things, the essence of things. And it's something that I've, as an artist has not only appealed to me but inspired me to kind of seek a way to express things in that way as well. I've actually had intention of going down to the Amerind Foundation. I've been talking to them about it for a couple years now, about visiting their Mimbres collection specifically. And so, this was kind of a project that came kind of out of sight. I mean it was unexpected. I was surprised. And I guess Gwen has expressed it like that, kind of like it's more than just an artistic journey. I feel like that's what it's been to me, it's been more. This is part of my journey. And I think I can sense that we're all that way in this room. That when we're looking and experiencing the landscape and when we're looking and experiencing the art. It's not just from our head or from our eyes. I think that we're all on our individual journeys as people. And I think we're all on our individual journeys as spiritual beings. And I think all of our journeys (are) at least collectively as artists, we share something that resonates in this art form and in this people. And I think when I visited the landscape what I was really touched by was that it had a lot in common with the landscape that I grew up in northern New Mexico. Hopi, it's a very different landscape. I saw Gila Wilderness when I was a little kid. And I saw a little picture of the dwelling. And I always wanted to go there because it looked like our ancestral village in Santa Clara, it's called *Puye*. And it's a cliff village. And up on top is another village. And when I saw this picture of Gila Wilderness, Gila Dwellings I said, "man that really looks like our home." And I wanted to . . . I was just curious. My grandfather, I spent a lot of time with him when I was young. And he was very much a teacher. And he was very much always looking to expand his own journey. And when we would travel between places he would always want to stop when there was a site. Anyway, I think that that desire (would) has also been there in me. And I've really wanted to not only look at the artwork but be able to somehow pay my own respect and my own communication with the people, with the ancestral people. This is my daughter, Epiphany. Anyway, where was I . . . Like I said I've always wanted to not only look at the artwork but also have a way to connect with the people. And this was really an amazing opportunity to do that. We walked in the same paths that they walked on. We passed by the same rivers that they passed by. We probably looked at the grandchildren of the turkeys. And so forth, the grandchildren of the fish. And so maybe we're grandchildren meeting grandchildren which is a really fun thought. I think like I said again, the landscape really touched me that way because it reminded me a lot of *Khapo Owinge*, Santa Clara Pueblo. To see the fish, to see the turkeys, even the antelope . . . not the antelope [the *ping kuwa*] . . . the bighorn sheep, the bighorn sheep, they . . .we don't have them but we have a lot of songs about them. And so that was really touching to me too, to see that in the pottery. I guess I feel right now moved. I feel inspired. And I'm really looking forward to continuing to look at the images. Mostly what I did as we did the review, I tried to draw throughout the review. As I would draw them, it just the simplest designs became very complicated. Complicated designs, you begin to see patterns in them. Going over the review made things very personal. You felt almost at times a connection with the painter or the potter. You could see strokes. You could see a fingerprint. But personally, I guess I would just really like to continue to look at the designs, to kind of work with what I've seen. And just I guess for lack of a better word just play with it a little bit, that's the wrong word but interact with it. Interact with the designs and see how they . . . see how they touch me, see what comes up. I don't have a real direction at this point but I have a lot of inspiration. Thank you. (Arakawa and Ito 2019)

Spencer Nutima's Description and Interpretation of the Mimbres Bowl G476-9

The shaman-like design was the pot that inspired Spencer's work for the exhibition. Spencer said,

Four inches deep. Probably seven and quarter, round, diameter. It has been heavily restored. It has brown color. On the outside it looks like it has been used to hide the cracks. It's quite a few cracks on this. Looks like the mouth is . . . bowl has been . . . seem to be repainted. But it has the same color as the thin lines. Five thin lines. You can tell where they have been blended together. And below that is about the same space in as between in-lines as a broad band. This is a human figure. It must have been great ruler because he has got those huge legs. But I notice his feet look like animal tracks. Would be a bear track. Hands are like lines. But they seem to be held in such a way that the thumbs are like this, when it's like this and the other like that. I don't know the arms are hard to hold that way. This figure looks like he has something on his face. I'm not sure if it is nose sticking out there. But he has got a sort of normal way of showing an eye, like a . . . almond shape. I think that dark area. I'm not sure about the opening and that not figure of what. And it's kind of square-ish head. And he got this I'm not sure what that is. Some

Figure 5.14.

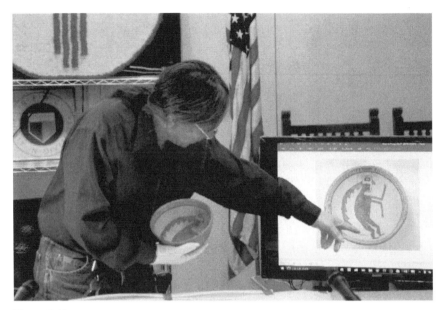

Figure 5.15.

kind of maybe feather design. It's got that. Like water design as well. Some of the dark pigment is . . . has been braided off. Somehow it has been like sanded off. Looks like this white here is maybe the . . . maybe original color of this, this part. Looks like it's been chipped here. This color goes over this edge. I'm not sure if this is the original color or somebody put the slip over it because it covers the cracks in some places. Although you can still see that crack, inside is hard to tell where the cracks are because they have repaired it. I don't know what kind of deity or whatever is trying to portray. If that, anyway, it's all I have to say about that. (Arakawa and Ito 2019)

Narrative of His Inspired Product

Hello, my name is Spencer Nutima. I'm from Old Orayvi. And I'm of the greasewood clan. I got my inspiration from the Mimbres pottery that had a figure similar to the carving that's on this plate. Also, the plate has Mimbres design on it, although it's a little bit different. My take on Mimbres design. But as you can see, the two points of the curved lines point to the central figure. It represents a continuum from the time that this figure was painted on the pottery. And I believe it probably represents the original, the first *katsina* that was ever . . . that came. And he was the Long Hair, even though it doesn't look like the Long Hair. But the Long Hair *katsina* was the first that was brought to us. So, it kind of painted in that style because of colors

Figure 5.16.

for his face and a kilt that he wears. So, I found out too that my clan comes from Mimbres people as well. So, I'm happy that I'm able to do this kind of work, I'm not saying what they call an elder. But I don't look at myself that way because I'm still doing my own person thing. So anyway, I'm happy to address you this way. And I hope you learn something and the happiness and prosperity in your life. (Arakawa and Ito 2019)

Narrative and Reflection Based on His Experience and Feelings during the Mimbres Valley Field Trip

My name is Spencer Nutima from Orayvi, Third Mesa in Arizona, Hopi tribe. I was asked to be this project for the Mimbres pottery. It's kind of excited that that would be able to do that. I had already been looking at the publications for a long time now. So anyway, so I was honored to do this. And so, touching the pots and looking at the actual thing give me more of an understanding of what the people were doing at that time when they were making the pottery and doing their designs. And so, after looking at those designs, I decided what I would do for my project. And I am going to do basically a katsina carving, top and the bottom. So, this whole piece will be probably 24 inches tall. I'm going to use the head of a *Salako*. Then his little feet at the bottom. And in between I'm going to use a pottery design as if you were looking at it straight on. This particular pot that I saw was more of like a small storage pot. So, it had . . . the opening was like so. So anyway, that would be the center of my piece. To me that would be like using it as a meditation point. And then looking into that void. You'll see that you don't see anything. So that's your focus. You try to empty your mind and go from there. So, we were taken up to the Mattock site where we're at now, the TJ site which was pretty cool. And the Gila Cliff Dwellings. I went there one time, probably six or seven years ago. And didn't really quite remember that well, but since I didn't have to drive, I got a feel about the landscape how it affected the lives of the people. And how they decided to live in these cliff houses. There were several occupations there. So that was a kind of a point for me because this particular site in particular, my clan, the greasewood clan claims. So, it was again a really inspirational to be in the place where my ancestors were. And so that's what sets the whole thing off. And so, I'm not sure what else I have to say. But this is a very cool spot where everybody had come and settled and through this Mimbres Valley and how there was so many villages. And they were almost so many miles apart. And they were using the landscape and not like over grazing or whatever you want to call it. So, they had a system of things going and of course there are the villages occupied at the same time but. And on the other hand, they had pretty good idea of how to use their resources. So that puts me in a good spot because I think we all should do that and respect our world, the Earth, other people, animals. And this great stream that we were sitting next to and the water that it provides for us. So, thanks for letting me be here. And I'll see you some other time maybe. (Arakawa and Ito 2019)

AUTHOR'S REFLECTIONS AND THOUGHTS

In my attempt to be an independent observer, I came to notice several aspects of this type of collaborative work. In this section, I address issues related to collaborative efforts between academic institutions and Native Americans— and most importantly, among the individuals representing those groups.

First, each Hopi artist was genuinely aware that their interpretations of Mimbres pottery designs were subjective and do not represent Hopi voices as a whole. Some archaeologists (e.g., Mason 2000) have denied the validity and applicability of integrating oral traditions into archaeological interpretations because it is seen as subjective. However, one of the important lessons to be learned from the Hopi artists is that interpretation, like the making of art, is a subjective and personal process. In response to archaeologists who are skeptical of subjectivity, I would argue that it is important for us as a field to recognize the subjectivity of our own process, which is one of the arguments I am trying to make in this book. It is important that these archaeologists recognize that Native American scholars, artists, and elders openly acknowledge their own limited voices. The Hopi artists taking part in this work were not attempting to provide definitive answers to all "deep meanings" visible in these designs, but they did aspire to share their thoughts and interpretations based on their own instincts, feelings, connections, aesthetics, and memories.

Additionally, all of the Hopi reviewers stated that their review of the Mimbres vessels would inform their own artistic techniques in the future. Several Hopi artists reflected on how the Mimbres potters manufactured their bowls—temper, firing process, and design layout—in comparison to contemporary Hopi pottery, and this, they stated, enhanced their own appreciation for and respect for ancient technologies and art. Aside from pottery manufacturing techniques, several of the Hopi artists compared the symmetrical or asymmetrical nature of painting designs and motifs inside Mimbres bowls with their own artistic styles and aesthetics, allowing them to incorporate "new" designs and motifs in their own contemporary art. The Hopi artists seemed to connect with the Mimbres potters' personal identity and with their own. Some Hopi artists were interested in discerning a specific maker's symbol. For instance, different numbers of framing lines were thought to indicate the makers' signatures.

Finally, by investigating Mimbres painting designs, the Hopi reviewers thought they may be able to reconnect the Mimbres potters' clan system and affiliation with contemporary ones. Some archaeologists (Adams 1991; Schaafsma 1974) have addressed the important concept of "katsina," which would be a spirit being, ancestors, clouds, rains, and/or fertility, in the American Southwest. Adams (1991) argues that although the katsina spirit or being, which consists of several different forms and performances (e.g., depicted in petroglyphs), has existed for over 4,000 years in the American Southwest since the introduction of maize to the area, some of the katsina forms might have been depicted in Mimbres bowls. In other words, the Mimbres people followed and practiced some kind of katsina rituals in the region around the AD 1000s to 1100s. Then, the belief was intensified and spread to the Salado culture area in the AD 1300s and then later to the Hopi and Zuni areas. If this premise is valid, there is a strong connection between the Mimbres and Hopis belief systems. Importantly, the Mimbres pottery designs and motifs would represent the origin of katsina belief. This further supports an idea that the contemporary Hopis continue to practice and use katsina forms and performances that might have been rooted and represented in Mimbres pottery designs and motifs.

Furthermore, it is important to highlight that each Hopi artist offers a different belief, perspective, and practice regarding sacred ancestral objects. When we encountered a Mimbres bowl with a punched hole (or a kill hole), one participant was able to touch and feel it. However, others were not. It is important for archaeologists to not generalize about cultural taboos based on one clan member's interpretations. Instead, archaeologists ought to obtain multifaceted interpretations from clan members across a wide demography. This is especially true regarding ritual knowledge that has been instilled in different clan members, as not all clan members share the same knowledge. Thus, I am not surprised that the deep meanings of certain Mimbres pottery designs have different interpretations demonstrated by the dynamic and multifaceted interpretations presented by the contemporary Hopi artists.

On the basis of this research, I sensed that the issue of "cultural affinity" (the attempt to discern who are the closest descendants of the Mimbres people) is not a major concern among Hopi artists. Historic Hopi migration often takes place by subclan, and each subclan continued to move around their landscape until they eventually arrived at the present-day Hopi homeland. This notion was captured by Spencer Nutima in his declaration that his greasewood clan was once settled near the Gila Cliff Dwellings National Monument according to his clan story, and now the clan is located in the current Hopi homeland (personal communication, October 1, 2017).

During our review process, I intuited that each Hopi artist was interested in the ancient designs and thus considered the adaptation and application of unique designs to their contemporary art. Some archaeologists, as well as some Native Americans, may find this to be a form of "cultural appropriation," meaning that if/when an outsider introduces "new ideas" and/or artistries to a traditional or Indigenous group, this introduction might cause an unexpected loss of original artistry. Based on our experience and conversation with the Hopi artists in this study, I contend that our effort to review ancient objects and our offer of collaborative research allows these individuals an opportunity to reconnect with their heritage through these ancient objects and is significantly valuable. As scholars, we benefit from understanding the multifaceted interpretations of the Mimbres pottery designs, and in turn the Hopi artists are exposed to innovative and creative ideas for their own contemporary art.

In addition to both archaeologists and Native Americans benefiting from this type of collaborative work, each Hopi artist became more aware of what traditional Hopi artistry is and what it is not. When they create their own sacred, traditional objects, they now have additional information by which they can separate their own traditional art from their non-traditional artworks.

Throughout this collaborative work, I also came to recognize that it was important for the artists to be able to communicate in Hopi (their native language) with one another or even myself if necessary. During the interview process, there were several occasions when Gerald and Ramson shared their thoughts and feelings about certain Mimbres pottery designs in Hopi because it allowed them to communicate ideas that were not directly translatable in English. Although these words were transcribed in English, the Hopi word often has a nuanced and complex meaning.

Given that our subject matter was pottery, I thought it necessary to have at least one individual who was knowledgeable about traditional pottery manufacture and design (in this case, Gwen). We also felt that it was important to have at least one participant with knowledge of Hopi arts and aesthetics who is well-versed in the larger art scene and aesthetics (e.g., Western arts and aesthetics). As one attempts to understand their own arts and aesthetic, it is necessary to reflect on their own artistic perspective by comparing and contrasting with that of others. A comparative approach is thus important when one wants to better understand one's own. Without this reflection and objectivity, an artist can only understand their own arts and aesthetics and not those of other artists. For this study, Ramson provided an excellent comparative perspective, particularly when considering concepts related to Western art and aesthetics while reviewing potential deep meanings of Mimbres pottery designs.

On the basis of this collaborative work with the Hopi artists, where I elicited their interpretations based on their cultural and artistic knowledge, which is quite different from archaeologists' systematic and objective descriptions and interpretations of archaeological objects, I advocate for listening to and incorporating Native Americans' voices when interpreting the archaeological record. Their voices are insightful, vibrant, and multifaceted, and I argue that archaeologists should patiently, and respectfully, listen to Native Americans' voices. By so doing, we can delve into the rich contextualization of an object, and enhance the narrative of human history and prehistory, through a close connection between archaeologists and Source Community members.

One of the important takeaways from this project was that it created an opportunity for the Hopi artists to engage in dialogue about their interpretations. While they didn't always agree, the artists gained insights from each other and were open to considering each other's perspectives. Importantly, it was an opportunity for them to listen to each other and in some cases become more aware of how their personal experiences (e.g., clan identities) shaped their interpretations in ways that were very different. In this same spirit, this book is an attempt to correlate different archaeological methodologies that don't necessarily agree with each other or have access to the same sorts of knowledge. Before we do this larger correlative work in the conclusion, in the following chapter I will show how Native interpretations should not be limited to the observation of the artifacts themselves. To do this, we will look at Native Science (or Indigenous ways of knowing) and how relationships to landscapes can inform interpretations.

1. http://ifm.minpaku.ac.jp/hopi

2. The reviewing process was funded by JSPS Grant-in-Aid for Young Scientists (A): Source Community Utilization of Ethnological Collections for Information Sharing in Japanese Museums (26704012) by Atsunori Ito, and JSPS Fund for the Promotion of Joint International Research (Fostering Joint International Research): Source Community Utilization of Ethnological Collections for Information Sharing in Japanese Museums (Fostering Joint International Research) (15KK0069) by Atsunori Ito. The exhibition was funded by two Southwest and Border Cultures Institute (SBCI) grants by Fumi Arakawa from NMSU.

3. The workshop was also supported by the Southwest and Border Cultures Institute (SBCI) grant from NMSU.

Chapter 6

Native Science

Jim Enote and Octavius Seowtewa

Indigenous ways of knowing have much to teach archaeologists about Mimbres pottery design. Jim Enote, a Zuni elder, who identifies with the Mimbres people, shares his thoughts on pottery making as a cultural practice:

> [I]t's important to remember watching my grandma make pottery and painting them. While she wasn't that totally explicit, but she understood it was things that represented being *witness* to something but also a matter of *hope* because you saw those clouds and those certain kinds of clouds only appear in the summertime and those summertime clouds bring rain it's something you hope for but it's also something you witness. Those birds that are around water whether it's before the rain or you see them around springs and what areas are canyons you find them there, you're witness to that and you always hope that the water is going to be there, and so in that it's both being witness to something and hope and hope is cosmology . . . I mean this is a time when these pieces were made; this is a time when you were living on the razor's edge of life. You know you're cold at night; you're waiting for the sun to come up; you're thirsty; you hope and look for water; you're hungry; you grow food; it's all these things, and you didn't have writing, and you're concerned with realism, but you put that expression that witness and that hope into this piece. (personal communication, October 19, 2019)

This chapter draws on conversations with two Zuni elders—Jim Enote and Octavius Seowtewa—in order to demonstrate how Native Scientists might approach the interpretation of the landscapes and artifacts that we are attempting to interpret in this book. Significant to their interpretation is how they challenge and negotiate interpretations offered and imposed by Western archaeologists.

Octavius Seowtewa is the head medicine man for the Newekwe/Galaxy medicine society and also a member of the Eagle Down medicine society. He is a supervisor for the Zuni Cultural Resources Advisory Team (ZCRAT). Octavius has been involved with numerous museum projects not only in the United States but also in Japan and in the Netherlands. He has reviewed an innumerable amount of Zuni cultural remains at museums for over twenty years. Since he is the head of the ZCRAT, he and his advisory groups have actively been involved in NAGPRA consultations with various federal and state agencies as well as with museum personnel.

Jim Enote is a Zuni tribal member and CEO of the Colorado Plateau Foundation. His services for the past forty years include work with natural resources, cultural heritage resources, philanthropy, and arts assignments for many organizations, such as UNESCO, International Secretariat for Water, National Geographic Society, US Bureau of Indian Affairs, US National Park Service, Zuni Tribe, and several major charitable foundations, museums, and universities. Jim and Octavius have worked together on research for several collections, and they are considered experts in the review of cultural objects as well as in landscape studies.

Native Americans have explicitly advocated for different ontologies and metaphysics that contrast with Euro-American perspectives regarding archaeological productions and interpretations. By sharing the perspectives and narratives of two Zuni elders based on their first-hand experiences at Mimbres sites in Gila National Forest, New Mexico, I hope to show how Indigenous ways of being and knowing are connected to a personal relationship with a landscape that is not available to Western or Eastern archaeologists.

The inclusion of Native American narratives regarding a particular landscape is meant to redress the historical exclusion of contemporary Native perspectives in the interpretation of prehistoric sites and surrounding landscapes. This inclusiveness of multivocal meanings in a particular landscape allows us to step out of the Western academic means of interpretation and enhance archaeological research.

In comparison to the multivocal studies in Chapter 5, this chapter focuses more on the topic of landscape studies, in that the elders directly observed the particular landscape by direct experience without looking at curated artifacts (e.g., Mimbres pottery bowls). These elders also inquired and exchanged their thoughts regarding the connection between the ancient groups and the Zunis as well as other Pueblo groups, and the lifestyles and beliefs of these people who inhabited the Gila National Forest. In the following sections, I will begin by situating the term Native Science (or Indigenous ways of knowing) and then discuss what we did for an archaeological collaborative work in the Mimbres region with Zuni elders in October 2019 and February 2020 and how the Zuni elders perceived and thought about the two archaeological sites and their surrounding landscape.

NATIVE SCIENCE

Native Science is a term used to recognize and respect Indigenous ways of knowing.[1] The term was coined by Gregory Cajete (2000, 3), who proposed Native Science as "a way of understanding the world, a story of how things happen, a way that human beings have evolved to try and explain and understand existence in time and space and relationships vis-à-vis the natural processes of the world." Cajete also argues that knowledge acquired by Native American people has a different source than that created from a Western perspective. To produce knowledge, Native Science uses metaphors consisting of multi-leveled and multi-layered symbols. Therefore, to understand Native Science, it is crucial to decode layers of meaning embedded in symbols.

In general, according to the Native Science perspective, symbols are used linguistically to depict structures and relationships to places inhabited by Native people now and in the past. This further indicates that landscapes are crucial ways for Native Americans to connect and understand multi-layered meanings about a particular place. The important concept of "places" (or landscape) is explicitly declared by Cajete (2000, 36), saying "Indigenous people's science is grounded on an understanding of perspective and orientation. All things are related and interconnected, everywhere and at all times, and understanding this is necessary to apprehend what Native people did as they related to living in a particular natural place."

Criticism of Native Science (Indigenous Ways of Knowing)

Native Science has become an important development in archaeological research (e.g., Atalay 2012). In particular, Native Science addresses one of the criticisms of multivocality by removing archaeologists as mediators and/or principal investigators of archaeological research. As a practice, Native Scientists ask their own questions and conduct research for their purposes. However, one of the limitations of Native Science is that it does not necessarily produce systematic and empirical knowledge for non-Native archaeologists. Further, for Native Science to be an Indigenous way of knowing, it requires peer-review by Indigenous peoples.

These characteristics of Native Science present several issues for non-Native archaeologists. First, since the majority of North American archaeologists are non-Native scholars, they are in practice excluded from Native productions of knowledge. Second, and in response to their exclusion, another limitation is that non-Native archaeologists might argue that Native Americans' knowledge is already included in archaeological records (e.g., multivocality), and therefore there is no need for Native Americans to develop their own field (a fifth element, i.e., Native Science or Indigenous archaeology). Finally, non-Native archaeologists might argue that not all Native Scientists should be recognized as authorities on ancient artifacts or cultural groups (i.e., regardless of descent groups) just because they are Native.

Although these critiques are important to consider when North American archaeologists attempt to interpret abstract materials (e.g., artifacts and landscapes), this does not mean that it is impossible for archaeologists to incorporate Indigenous ways of knowing in their research. Under the nomenclature of Native Science or Indigenous ways of knowing, what follows is my attempt to collaborate with two Zuni elders in a shared effort to interpret ancient landscapes in the Gila National Forest.

MIMBRES LANDSCAPE STUDIES IN THE GILA NATIONAL FOREST

The landscape studies with two Zuni elders had three goals. First, it was an opportunity to help the Zuni elders reconnect with their ancestors who once inhabited the land. Currently, they live in the Zuni Reservation, which lies in the northwestern part of New Mexico approximately 200 miles from the Gila National Forest. While the Zuni elders recognize this area as ancestral land, they are not personally intimate with it. The second goal was to gain the insights and narratives that seeing the landscape for themselves might offer us as a means of interpretation. Finally, the landscape studies allowed us to listen to the Zuni's critiques and thoughts as Native Scientists on existing interpretations by archaeologists.

The Zuni elders began creating their own interpretations of the landscape, culture, and people, instead of depending on archaeological and ethnographic records that were originated by ethnographers in the late nineteenth and early twentieth centuries. This was firmly emphasized by these elders, who said that their involvement in this project was for the purpose of rewriting biased interpretations created by many ethnographers about the culture and history of Zuni. Both elders were interested in participating in this project because of this specific reason. Ultimately, this was one of the primary reasons they agreed to collaborate with us rather than to just experience the landscape on their own.

To achieve these goals and purposes, the two Zuni elders, Jorden Scott (a graduate student), three Gila National Forest personnel, and I visited one Classic Mimbres site (Twin Pines Village) and two rock art panels near

Figure 6.1. Jim Enote (left) and Octavius Seowtewa (center) share Zuni oral traditions as Jorden Scott (right) listens.

Chloride, New Mexico (Figure 6.1). During the field trip, we listened to the Zuni elders' voices and narratives regarding the landscape use by Mimbres people who inhabited the area from AD 1000 to 1150. In addition to the landscape study, Jorden Scott, one of my graduate students, inquired about the importance of symbols of swallows and swifts by the Zunis (Scott 2020). In the Mimbres Pottery Images Digital Database (MimPIDD), Scott found that the Mimbres people depicted a great amount of swallow and swift designs on their bowls. For her thesis research, to understand and reconstruct the meanings of these birds, she interviewed these Zuni elders.

When proposing this project, the two elders stated that they felt a strong connection with the people who inhabited the landscape of Gila National Forest in the past. Indeed, both elders had previously visited the area to hunt wild turkeys and elk, though they did not pay attention to archaeological sites and cultural resources prior to this project. To effectively record these elders' voices and narratives, the author initially received Institution of Research Board (IRB) approval from NMSU. While visiting Gila National Forest, a national forest employee used an audio device, transcribed the recordings, and created a documentary film.[2] The Gila National Forest employees, Jorden Scott, and I also visited these elders in Zuni one day to validate culturally sensitive descriptions, terms, and interpretations in the transcribed manuscript. During this visit, the Zuni elders also reflected on and shared their thoughts and perspectives about the landscape in Gila National Forest and provided us many additional interpretations of the area.

VOICES FROM NATIVE AMERICAN ELDERS

While visiting the Twin Pines Village site and two rock art panels near Chloride, I was thrilled to learn from these elders. Prior to this project, my perspectives on the landscape of the Gila National Forest were mostly drawn on a processual archaeological framework, using objective and scientific ways of understanding and reconstructing the past. For example, I intended to investigate questions such as: How far did ancestral groups need to travel to obtain water and other natural resources in a particular landscape? How far was the distance between one community and another community; and did the distance of these communities indicate a sense of territoriality or a competitive conflict environment? While answers to these questions can inform us on the logistics of survival, they do not give us insight into how the people lived and experienced the land. As bearers of ancestral knowledge, the Zuni elders were my mentors and teachers regarding landscape studies and histories. Not only could they relate to the land in intimate ways, but they could also interpret and communicate messages that their ancestors left behind.

In this chapter, I have organized what I learned to correspond with the topics of previous chapters, including culture history, processual archaeology, post-processual archaeology, and multivocality. Each subtitle is my attempt to code or organize what I learned from the Zuni elders. While the act of coding is subjective and the product of my biases and interests, my intent is not to manipulate what I learned but rather to make the conversations more accessible and to prepare us for the focus on correlative archaeology in the conclusion of this book. Importantly, while interviewing the Zuni elders, Jorden Scott and I mostly took ourselves out of the dialogue because we wanted to focus on their insights instead of on ours. In addition, this narrative also includes the Zuni elders' thoughts, feelings, and perceptions pertaining to the heritage of Gila National Forest revealed by their questioning each other. Lastly, I have framed the dialogue with the Zuni elders by situating the discussion in a larger context and then extrapolating some takeaways.

ON CULTURAL HISTORY

Rewrite and Redirect Their Histories

Both Zuni elders agreed that reconnecting to archaeological sites and arti-facts, features, and rock art is crucial for them to rewrite and redirect how archaeological, anthropological, and ethnographic records have been navigated and interpreted. This point by the elders can be applied to critiques for the definition and description of different cultural groups by culture history scholars in the past. Sources of anthropological and archaeological research have heavily relied on ethnographers' descriptions and interpretations in the nineteenth and twentieth centuries. These elders strongly believe that Source Community members' involvement in archaeological research will help academics redirect and correct what has been said and recorded by these early ethnographers. According to the two Zuni elders, these early ethnog-raphers often obtained inaccurate information from Zuni people in the past. Octavius said,

I am pretty sure that Jim can agree with me, that I always jump at the chance when people want to know about Zuni. Because even with Bunzel, Stevenson, and some of Cushings, the Zuni people did not want to give that information. They just wanted to get rid of that individual, so they lied to them. These individuals went out and wrote a book about it, and people read about them [it] and they think, Oh this is how Zuni is; this is how they are. No, they were not. It's just that our leaders, when these individuals barged in, they wanted to get rid of them. So now students are being informed about Zuni from those books and now that we're given the chance to actually be out here and talking about the importance of this place; of course, I'm going to jump at the chance to be here. (personal communication, October 19, 2019)

One of the issues these Zuni elders bring up is how knowledge produced by culture history scholars and ethnographers can be problematic. Further, because these productions are esteemed by academics, subsequent archaeo-logical work is often built on these works, which only exacerbates the prob-lem. As explained in Octavius's critique, Native Science or Indigenous ways of knowing would clarify and rewrite the inaccurate information obtained by early archaeologists and ethnographers.

Early Form as Humans

While looking at a few pictography designs near Chloride, the Zuni elders began sharing their emergence story. Octavius said,

Yes, there's petroglyphs down the Colorado River. Right below Lava Falls there's a petroglyph that identifies what we looked like when we emerged from the bottom of the Grand Canyon, how we were transformed into upright figures and then a trail going to the middle place. But the first figure has webbed hands and webbed feet and tail protrusions in the forehead and all of our oral history states that's how we looked when we first came out. Then the other one they don't have webbed hands; they're a little taller, and then there's a trail that goes to the circle in the middle place. So, what we see, what archaeologist's [descriptions of] anthropomorphic figures is what we actually looked like, and we see them everywhere. We saw some down in Deming on that walk; they had the figures there too. And then there's a figure on the Supai Formation [with webbed hands and feet is central to the Zuni emergence stories] that's how they looked; how they saw the evening and the morning star as the Ahayuda and then they came down to the bottom of the Grand Canyon they actually noticed that they didn't have legs. So, they have a figure with the head sometimes with earrings and dangling hands but no legs. You see them around San Juan, Grand Canyon, Walnut Canyon, and all the way to Deming. So, they're leaving that information behind. So that they will never forget how we were transformed and so those . . . and I saw this too . . . Jim, when you were shining the light, I see a figure here too. I see the head and the neck, hands, so that information is something they don't ever want to forget. How we were transformed; how we came out . . . (personal communication, October 19, 2019)

Octavius's commentary helps us understand that the Zunis have their own creation story and theories of journeys and migrations. This elucidates that the Zunis' origin story is not based on solely scientific evidence, but derived from knowledge passed down from generation to generation. The rock art depictions are real in that they communicate important messages for the Zunis as well as for other Native American tribes. Petroglyphs can be mediators between the modern-day Zunis and their ancestors; their messages connect Zunis to people in the past, present, and future.

In addition, when Jim asked Octavius this question: "What rock art have you seen in Mimbres country that really solidifies the relationship to Zunis today?" Octavius replied,

Yeah, actually I think that one sort of came late, and it is compared to what is called the mythical Phoenix; it comes back rejuvenated itself but the biggest petroglyph we've seen that are everywhere where people have traveled is the anthropomorphic figure, and I think some people call it the lizard man. But, it's how we emerged from the bottom of the Grand Canyon with webbed hands, webbed feet, tails protrusions in the forehead, and those are packed into a lot of these sites because even today our people do not want to forget how we emerged from the bottom of the Grand Canyon, and they left that information for us to come back and really talk about our connection to all of these places when we do find . . . within the site. So, it's kind of odd that people are calling it "the lizard man" because that's how we emerged, and there's a petroglyph that really ties into that history of our people, how we're changed. And I will direct it to follow the path, the trail to find the middle place. And that information is at the bottom of Grand Canyon where we emerged. It really ties us to a lot of these different places with the picture [pictograph and petroglyph] information I lived by our ancestors end up for some people . . . they call it art rock or art panel but for us it's our library to history for people within these areas. (personal communication, February 22, 2020)

Again, Octavius's commentary is a conviction that pictographs and petroglyphs found in an area are not just abstract images or data sources for when and where people lived. For the Zunis and other Native American groups, rock art is an important frame of reference for them to connect to the areas that their ancestors inhabited that provides documented accounts of their ancestors' experiences.

One People

Throughout this project, Octavius explicitly emphasized the important concept of "one people" held by many Pueblo groups in the past. He told us that he used to trace, identify, and determine where the ancestors of only the Zunis went and left their remains and signs, but his perception has changed. Now, he sees that cultural materials left behind were associated with all Pueblo people today. His perception reflects and criticizes how the concept of culture or culture group was created by culture history archaeologists in the past. Octavius said,

I'm pretty sure that the people were here like we mentioned yesterday that what they call the Mimbres are also a part of the Salado, the Mogollon, all these people were during that time were one people. It was the archaeologist that gave them all these different names. So, for us finding a shrine there and we definitely said it was Zuni. So, it really goes into what we've been saying about all these people were here at the same time with artifacts being so different. I found one that had a lot of mica in it and that mica is coming from . . . I mean the northern tribes are using that *tsu'haba* [mica]. So, getting all that information here. Just proves my point of our people being one . . . And I've been trying to get my Puebloan friends and brothers to make that statement saying that we are the same people. And I didn't really have any good point until we went to the Canyon of the Ancients. And worked there and it was their determination that there was 80,000 people there at that time. So, I asked the Hopis if they ever had 80,000 people. They said no. Zuni never had; Acoma never had. But if you combine all of the Pueblo people now, it'd probably be equal to that. So, coming to sites like this it's . . . and I did kind of joke around yesterday . . . because if Zuni comes here, and that was like 5–10 years ago, we would say "Oh this is all Zuni." Hopis would come in and make the same statement. "Oh this is all Hopi." But now with the artifacts, what studies have been done on points, artifacts, everything that was collected here, it points to all of us not just one group of people and I think that's why our culture and who we are is still being sustained because of what we learn from each other. (personal communication, October 19, 2019)

Octavius's comments above contradict how culture history scholars and other non-Native archaeologists have segregated ancient groups into multiple distinct groups. Octavius's point reminds us that ancient people were connected; people moved around and married in and out for over hundreds and thousands of years. Therefore, archaeologists should consider the concept of one common ancestry and focus more on discoveries of similarities rather than differences in archaeological records.

Similar to the perception above, while Jorden Scott was showing some Mimbres pottery designs, Octavius identified cloud symbols, saying,

We talked about the cloud symbols. Acoma talks about the same cloud symbols. Hopi uses the same and working with these individual tribes, it just wanted me to maybe talk to them about wanting to have our elected leaders to come up with a resolution, saying that because of our shared identity that our people were probably together a long time ago. And looking at some of the well Mimbres . . . we already see a lot of Zuni symbols in there. (personal communication, October 19, 2019)

By looking at the designs in Mimbres artifacts, Octavius could identify with them because they resembled the cloud symbols that are used by the Hopis and other Pueblo groups. Octavius's commentary contradicts culture history's way of categorizing ancient groups in the past. Simply put, Octavius contended that all ancient groups were united in the past; thus, they should not be separated into particular groups based on archaeological findings, particularly by using designs and motifs of artifacts and rock art.

The Counter-Mapping Movement

At the Twin Pines Village site, the whole landscape is crucial for the Zuni elders to understand and reconnect with people or ancestors who inhabited the area. Jim prefers to refer to a sacred "place" rather than a sacred site. The sacred place encompasses not only a particular archaeological site but also water, agricultural fields, terraces, and other features—a whole place. The Zuni elders also told us how important the peaks of mountains and high peaks are in a particular landscape. Octavius mentioned that there is a shrine on the top of Eagle Peak near Reserve in New Mexico, and the shrine protects the Zuni and other Pueblo people. Jim was also interested in how these peaks and ridgetops were used for the purpose of communication among villagers in the past.

On the basis of the conversation about the landscape study, we asked Jim about his counter-mapping project. It is a project that produces maps based on Indigenous people's and Native Americans' knowledge and perspectives regarding a landscape. This approach indeed opposes how processual archaeologists attempt to understand the relationship between environment and humans in a particular area based on positivistic perspectives. Jim coherently discussed his view of the project, saying,

So, I think an important thing to think about with maps. Now what some people would say that maps are very defined, as I said they're very arbitrary—this is ours, this is yours. That's why we survey areas to the exact dimension and points, and but I think if you think about the long long long term as Native people have and still do is that boundaries already in five hundred years what you have on your survey forms may be a lot different in five hundred years, and people today will take five hundred years; let's can't even get my head around that doesn't mean anything to me, but when you think, we've been here for several thousands of years. We live further north at some time, but it was hot we were living for the north, when it got colder, we moved further south. And so, it is for us to think in the long-term I guess in the scheme of things no long-term, but it was cooler up here; we were further south Mimbres country. When it was warmer down there, we moved further north where there were a people were moving all the time . . . just movement of people is just part of the human experience of people are moving all the time. And I think maps would be part of telling that history, will be part of documenting, and it doesn't have to be exact. Kind of ways that we would think as a map being specific in mentioning sites, and exact locations, and such all those are helpful, but I think what would be where a role of counter-mapping with play or map part would play is let's listen to the history of the oral histories and then illustrate those oral histories of place, so oral history and art coming together around the idea of place is what this is about, so I think that's what it was to play an important role. I think I've worked with other tribes and other people around the world that are interested in the idea of color mapping and map art. And I guess in one sense I'm sort of a map activist and that one thing I tell them is yes, "you know; do it if that's what you want to do, how do you want to use these maps to assert your ideas of place, and why or what do you want to protect, or what issue do you want to call out with mapping" . . . but I would always say be careful too because remember maps are so powerful, and you don't want to create a map that's going to be detrimental to your idea in the future. I don't create a map that says this is our reservation or this is our land; this is the extent of our place when in one hundred years later your ancestors, I'm sorry your children and grandchildren so on may say well actually that's not the extent of our lands. But you made our map that said that's the extent of our lands, you don't want that to hurt your future. And the other thing is really what I forgot to mention is when you're doing mapping, what's at the front of it to think about when you're doing mapping is what not to map because there's some things in some places that everybody doesn't have to know about their histories or . . . some important sacred places that not everybody has to know about whether it's the history of that place or whether it's a place that's important to only a few people by gender or for cultural reasons. That some people have access and know about some places for a reason and not everybody has to know about that. So, one thing is like remembering first, what not to map but when you have consensus and all people are really have come together around the idea of creating map art or counter maps, then you can start moving forward. But I would spend time to meet with the right people, people the community with standing, people in the community who have the authority, and such, and then start the kiva which you want to map. Before just going out making cultural maps, counter maps, and things like that and have it hurt you in the future. You don't want to do that, so all this really confronts again this idea of different ways of going. And I think that's something that Native people need to begin to assert, and we're just beginning to do that. So counter maps are just part of that movement I have been doing and working on projects since I was very young, but now I'm at an age where I'm not going to do projects so much anymore because projects at the beginning and end. I'm more interested in a movement because of what this counter-mapping is doing. (personal communication, February 22, 2020)

Jim's commentary contradicts how non–Native American archaeologists often want to define culture areas by looking at temporal and spatial distributions of different artifacts, architectural types, burial practices, and other archaeological evidence. As Jim said, maps are powerful because each person, community, and/or entity conceptualizes a particular landscape differently. This further indicates that the cultural boundaries created by culture history scholars would be different from how Native Scientists look at a particular landscape or culture area.

ON PROCESSUAL ARCHAEOLOGY

Ecology/Landscape

At the end of the field trip with these Zuni elders, I, as a processual-trained archaeologist, asked about ecology/landscape within the Diamond Creek drainage area. I asked questions such as: What do you think of how the ancestral people used this landscape? What kind of resources did these people procure and utilize? Both elders responded to the questions, commenting on aspects in ways similar to the interests of processual archaeologists. Jim said,

I think, first I was drinking some water because I was thirsty, so of course to be living here first thing is where the water is. I mean that is something especially important to the Puebloan people. I have some friends that are Navajos. They're good friends of mine, but they always talk about—almost bragging—that "we haul water from far away." But then, they also say, begrudgingly, "we have to haul water all the time." And I would tease them and say well that's what you get for living so far away from the water. Pueblo people live where the water is at. And that's why our ancestors were here. Water first. First of all was water. And so, there's the drainages, the confluences here. The drainages were the highways—the first pathways. And they came up and they probably saw standing water I would guess, or cottonwoods and the spring and say well, there's water, let's have a drink here. And probably someone said this looks like good soil too. This is a nice flat area, there is water, let's stay here, camp for a while. And then somebody probably walked up here and said there is a nice flat spot up there. And then also said there is plenty of firewood. And probably started getting to work and somebody said there is a whole bunch of these nice straight beams over here. Not necessarily ponderosa pine but maybe some of these alligator junipers and others, and said there is a good supply of that. And so, there's building materials. But because I am a farmer myself, I'm clued into the water and the valley here which would be good for growing food. And then this palisade up here it's nice and flat, it's up above the cold in the winter because cold air is going to settle down in the lower areas, it's going to be a big difference even between here and the bottom and this will be a little bit warmer. And you have a little bit of a windbreak from the trees up here I think. I'm just thinking about the landscape, it's a good place to live. (personal communication, October 19, 2019)

Jim's commentary supports how processual archaeologists look at a particular landscape. He explicitly suggested that physiology and topography of landscape is important for ancient people to determine where the ideal place to inhabit is. This can be aligned with processual archaeologists' perspectives that focus on the relationship between humans and their environment, and how a particular landscape can provide abundant or scarce resources for ancient people.

Visceral Landscape

Since the Twin Pines Village site is located in a confluence of the Diamond Creek drainage and the headwaters of the Gila River, I also asked a question about whether these Zuni elders have heard an oral history or myth about headwaters (source of water).

Jim explicitly reflected on his thoughts about the headwaters, saying,

Well, you know there's a lot of—our ancestors were navigating the landscape of this world a lot. And so, they didn't just go across country. You wouldn't go up and down these hills to get somewhere. You would follow the easiest path and often it would be through these drainages, but also you would go from water source to water source. And from the Grand Canyon to where we live . . . And I'm sure it'd be very similar to here is that the drainages are like umbilical cords that connect us back to places. So, these drainages they're all sort of a visceral landscape and they connect us, one place to another—the springs. And Octavius knows this way more than I do, but those songs that are just about this spring and that spring. And they're also maps of how we got to be where we are. So, I don't know of this one but I'm sure the people lived here probably—there were songs about how they got here. And without knowing those . . . but we can see them also, in some ways, in the ceramics. You start looking at the clay, where did this clay come from? And even seeing images of wetland birds painted on pots you say, well, there must've been wetlands there. Or there must have been a spring or a wet spot there. So, in a sense our maps are in all these things, they are in our ceramics, they're etched in stone, they're woven into textiles, and they're in prayers and songs. (personal communication, October 19, 2019)

Jim's commentary above supports processual archaeologists' systematic and objective approaches in terms of landscape studies. For example, using Geographic Information System (GIS) techniques, processual archaeologists can figure out a shortest path from one site to another by calculating the energy expenditure of each individual. The technique would offer the result that drainages might be the key aspect for traveling between one site and another due to the low elevation and moderate slope in the landscape. Also, water sources, which are generally located in low elevations, would be an important variable for the analysis.

In turn, Jim reminded us that archaeologists often overlook the cultural importance of songs that are connected to particular places and the mnemonic acts that allow communities to remember events that took place in the area. This further implies that only Native Americans might be able to trace back and connect a particular landscape by retrospectively reconnecting memories in the past.

Born during the Big Snowstorm

Although the Zuni elders provided similar perspectives regarding descriptions and interpretations of landscapes by processual archaeologists, Octavius offered different ways of knowing about the time period. He said,

Well, there's all these different materials here. There's basalt; a chunk here. One there, I've seen some there. And then a lot of these materials were brought in for a specific reason and use. So, any information that comes from here would be very important to us because we live close to a basalt source, and we have a lot of use for it. Just the environment itself is ideal—water. The lookout, the area where they build their homes . . . even to this day would be ideal for somebody to be living here. And making use of the land. So even without any engineering degrees or any other degree of horticulture, science or anything, they manage to survive. And this was passed down from generation to generation. And it goes back so many years, people were asking us, "Well can you be definite when," and "the exact date?" And our people didn't come up with the dates. They, I think, I referenced my grandmother, I asked her when she was born. And she said that when there was—they told me—I was born during the big snowstorm. And it's not really specific but that's the reasoning that used for important events. Yes, so it was very gratifying to come to a place like this because it's a place where they survived. A place where we can reference and come back to and reconnect back to our people were here. And I was asking Jim, we need find a place to leave an offering because we need to reconnect back. Found this there [holding up crystal] and of course definitely is going to be—and I was looking around, and there was a square box that could be—*Adesh Kwinne* [in Zuni]—so it can go back there and leave an offering because when we come to an area, we don't just walk away. [We] want to make sure that we do leaving offering for reconnection back. And so here before we leave, we're going to have to do that. (personal communication, October 19, 2019)

Octavius also said, "So all of these were very important and like I mentioned, everything that you find in ancestral sites, the use that they got from all of these materials can still come here to present Zuni and still hear the same instruments and the same things used in ceremony" (personal communication, February 22, 2020).

According to Octavius's commentary, Native Science, or the Indigenous way of knowing, has a different relationship to the landscape than do non-Native archaeologists' perspectives. One major difference is the concept of time. When processual archaeologists, for example, attempt to figure out the event of migration, they aim to understand its specific time period using the results of ceramic seriation and radiocarbon and tree-ring analyses. In contrast, as Octavius indicated, Native Americans generally use reckonings related to important events. Their perspectives regarding the past time would be arbitrary, but these events were real. In short, many events that took place in the past by Native Americans' perspectives would be described and interpreted by a different conceptualization of time, and songs and dances, which modern-day Native Americans continue to engage in and practice, allow them to communicate and remember the past events.

ON MULTIVOCALITY

Just to Say "We Do Not Know"

Some archaeologists believe that Source Communities sometimes create their own stories based on their own perspectives and experiences, and these perspectives generate biases pertaining to the past human behaviors. It is, however, important to point out that these Zuni elders acknowledge the issue, and while looking at rock art panels, Jim explicitly said,

And then see, what else is there. Then in this part of this panel here we weren't sure about these. And I think this is important and that we are saying that sometimes Native people are in these situations and they feel like somebody's finally listening to me and they'll talk, maybe even stretch things a little bit, but what we found is more important for us is just to say if we don't know; we don't know, rather than to try to stretch it. So that's something that we are very attentive to. Just to say we don't know. Because it doesn't help in the future if that goes into recording and in 50 years or 100 years a young Zuni, then later an older Zuni, says, "Well, Octavius said it was this. Jim Enote said it was this." And, well they were really bullshitting. Because in the future Zuni people might know even more later. And up here we weren't sure what these were. We feel that these could be four-sided diamonds. (personal communication, October 19, 2019)

Jim's commentary explicitly addressed that the elders offered their own descriptions and interpretations of rock art designs based on their experience, knowledge, and identity. This further suggests that each Native American elder or individual would provide a different kind of knowledge and information regarding archaeological interpretations. This statement would support how post-processual and multivocality scholars aim to interpret archaeological remains, such as objects and landscapes, based on multiple reasonings by diverse individuals.

Imposing on One's Image/Ideas

When Jorden Scott provided several bird images which were very small and difficult for them to see, the elders still attempted to describe and interpret them. While reviewing these images, Jim taught us how the collaborative work between Source Communities and academics should take place. He offered one example, saying,

And well not to put myself on a pedestal, but organizing and especially thinking about different knowledge systems is something I do very naturally. One thing we did last night was, Jorden was showing us images of birds on ceramics that she was saying were swallows. And this is not disparaging in any way. But this is I think an important fork in the road, we see this in museums with archaeology and other things where people say we want to show you these images of raccoons or of these pottery types that are canteens and things or musical instruments whether it's out in the field or even in the museum; they'll say the catalog says that these are this, so why don't you take a look at the catalog and then we'll look up objects or the place and really what that's doing is disciplining us to start thinking that way already. It's starting to be biasing us to think it's that way. So, it's easier for us to say, "oh yeah," that is what it is. Whereas what we think that the field should be doing and we got into some of that last night because it was a good conversation. It's like for example—like I would not have said this is an owl. I would've said I'm going to bring you to this place and show it to you and to say "what do you think," and so that we would just with a fresh perspective study it and tell you what we think. So, it's already kind of biasing us in a way. Do you know what I'm saying? So, I think this is just a good fork in the road because for so many years ethnography, anthropology, and archaeology have been doing that saying, we want to show you what we think they are. And then many Native people will say okay because there is a little bit of power thing going on. Well, they know these things, so let's think of it in that frame of mind versus like let's go look at these things and tell us what you think, that's fresher that way. (personal communication, October 19, 2019)

According to Jim's commentary above, the problem is multivocality is often mediated by someone else's objectives and goals (e.g., archaeologists, cultural anthropologists, and ethnographers). Indeed, when I initiated this project with Jim and Octavius, Jim was explicitly concerned about the problem with multivocality, especially how non-Native scholars impose their own questions. Because of these reasons, when we visited two rock art panels and the Twin Pines Village site, we initially let the Zuni elders take a look at petroglyphs and pictographs and the landscape in and surrounding the site by themselves. Jim's comments are vital and an excellent lesson for non-Native archaeologists to recognize and reconsider their methodology. His message especially helps non-Native archaeologists to be careful when American archaeologists consult with Native Americans (e.g., the NAGPRA consultations and documentations).

Collaboration

I also asked the elders about collaborative work, especially between archaeologists and Source Communities. Since I have been directing summer archaeology field schools in Gila National Forest since 2015, I wanted to know how the collaboration with Native Americans can be achieved. I was also interested in how to balance the power of scholarship between academics and Source Communities. In other words, how will both academic institutions and Source Communities be able to gain mutual benefits by carrying out collaborative work? Octavius discussed the importance of collaboration, especially participation in field research with archaeologists, saying,

I think it's very important that the Zuni people are part of this because what they identify, what they can give interpretations to or their expert opinion on what these items are. Because it comes back to us going back to the lab and looking at it. We don't really know the context of where it came from and it takes away the importance of this one artifact if we're just looking at it through a bag or microscope, then it takes away from the importance of actually where came from. And that's what we've been doing with Denver Museum of Nature and Science. What they might consider site trash would be an artifact. Conglomerates and concretions, even the smallest round rock, if it's found in the house it was used for a reason—a reason why it was found there. It just didn't come off the wall and roll in there. So any . . . and I think it's turning around now, that we're given an opportunity to be part of even if just the start and the end of the project itself, that we will be able to be a part of it and I think it would really give it more weight to your project if it states that the Zuni advisory team members were here on these dates and this is information they gave us and that way it would be—have more information than if we come back or if we go to your lab and look at items and not really know the reason why it was left there or where they actually found it. (personal communication, October 19, 2019)

Jim added,

I think working with students and in particular Native students and tribes or pueblos like Zuni, Acoma or whatever, the ones related, would help build the capacity of the students to do the work in the future . . . to help represent us in the future you know. Not to be fatalistic but Octavius and I aren't going to be around forever so those young people need to be informed. And to be equipped to represent us in the future . . . it's about showing that true collaboration is possible, and I don't mean just like a phone call or meeting but actually co-laboring towards a mutual agreement. Something . . . a plan that has some mutual outcome. Like a Pueblo or Octavius and I or something work with you and say you know what we would want out of this—what we would really like to see out of this. If we are going to partner with you on this, this is what we would like to see as the outcomes—for us. And you have your outcomes. And then we both then collaborate to those mutual outcomes. So that's the third thing. I mean I've been on both sides of the fence for many years. Raising money and also in giving. And so, there's . . . to think about how to do this with a real strategic way is one . . . how you're engaging with the Native community, and how you are influencing the field and how you are contributing to the field. (personal communication, October 19, 2019)

Both Octavius's and Jim's commentaries are vital for archaeologists to recognize a mutually beneficial collaborative work with Native Americans. Multivocality has been becoming popular and practiced by non-Native archaeologists in the United States, but non-Native archaeologists should be aware of the existence of multiple steps in its methodology. If archaeologists begin their multivocal and collaborative work after research designs and/or research questions are carried out without consultation with Native Americans, it does not help us develop the mutual benefits of a true collaborative work. Archaeologists also should be aware that working and collaborating with Native American youth would be another important element for continuing and developing a multivocal and collaborative work with Native Americans in the future.

Interviewed by Themselves

Finally, Jorden Scott, two others, and I visited Octavius and Jim in Zuni on February 22, 2020. The consultation meeting had two initiatives. One was to review all documented materials with them and deal with culturally sensitive information. This was conducted by Jorden Scott and me. The other initiative was put forward by Jim and Octavius, who wanted to continue the conversation by asking each other questions regarding their experience in Gila National Forest. I believe this happened because I did not ask sufficient questions while interviewing them at the rock art and Twin Pines Village sites in October 2019. In other words, I believe that Jim generously wanted to help us get more and ensure that they spoke to issues that they felt were important. This demonstrates the need for Native Americans to work with Native Americans in terms of the advancement in multivocality and Native Science.

Jim asked Octavius about potential Zuni names farther south (the Mimbres region). Jim asked, "So, there is physical evidence of Zuni's time down in Mimbres country. There is still place names; there is obviously still animals and birds that we have to go south to get them and the young people here in Zuni, especially, are missing some of this knowledge. What would you like this new generation and those to come to know about this relationship to Mimbres?"

Octavius answered,

Just having information like that out there and especially with hopefully this new video as short as it may be, hopefully we can persuade people who can't visit sites but also have the respect because for us it's still a living history, and it's not a place that has ever been forgotten; it's just that some of these places are now federal land owned properties or private properties, and it keeps us out from revisiting our ancestors. But when we come to work with different groups, different museums, federal agencies, that we come to work with these agencies we get a chance to come and visit with our ancestors when we go back to the sites, so our young children here are very eager to learn about their history, and I tell them it's not just this little piece of land that we called the reservation. There's more lands out there that our ancestors walked, that they stopped, they raised families and had the same ceremonies that we do have here, and I think that's one of the big things that has never been put out to our Zuni youth, and now working with the high school and the middle school that I'm actually given an opportunity to talk about all of our histories just beyond our reservation borders. (personal communication, February 21, 2020)

Because of the discussion above, Jim summarized what they thought about the Mimbres region and posed another question to Octavius,

So, we've seen here in our own oral histories, our relationship to Mimbres country—what people in archaeology called Mimbres country—and so we are now because we have more mobility and we have the relationships with different agencies . . . we're able to have more access to these places, so it's starting to reaffirm our oral history that tells us we are connected or closer to Mimbres than we really have ever known. Now what would you say to people in scholarship at universities or people working in federal agencies or state agencies who are studying their rich culture; what would you say to them about now we have our own history, we have more access; how can scholarship begin to build on the evidence of our relationships? Let's, well, there's lots of things like some of those points you know now we're seeing some of the ground penetrating radar and there are things that we look at it and say, "Yeah that's helpful, we didn't have that, we didn't have access to it," so scholarship is starting to help us put our knowledge together with white peoples' knowledge just like bringing two different knowledge systems together. So, what would you tell scholarship for those students . . . how was academics . . . how would their studies help build this evidence and tell the story of its history? (personal communication, February 21, 2021)

Octavius responded,

I've been working with an individual that was just out there studying turquoise and for us it's very important . . . the use of turquoise not just for adornment, to wear for ceremonies or every day, but also it's a main component to our offerings as chips of turquoise. And I wouldn't have known how turquoise is identified where they came and asked me for help and about the use of turquoise here in Zuni . . . and what I learned from him was the isotope studies that are done and they can pinpoint exactly where that turquoise came so scholarship academia now . . . they're helping us to identify even some of the turquoise that are found here that has been excavated . . . they can identify exactly where they came from. The research that he did here in Zuni for the middle village when they were excavating, they found turquoise, and there was three sources that were identified, and also some turquoise that came from El Morro was the Cerrillos mine . . . and then there are two mines in what is now Apache country in the White Mountains, so actually had an opportunity to go to all three of those mines because I referenced that when our ancestors do go and collect material, they don't just go ahead and steal it . . . they have to leave an offering, and so there has to be a shrine; there has to be an offering place. And we did find one up in the White Mountains and we actually collected turquoise on the surface so that was the same thing that our ancestors did without working with [so head quest] . . . he passed away . . . he was doing, I was doing a study and without his information and his knowledge even to this day we wouldn't know where those turquoise came . . . the students out there go into different fields . . . different study, there's a lot of information, a lot of things that we still need to strengthen and really put our Zuni history tie to these places if they do more research of . . . even where the mica came from, even where the basalt came from, I'm pretty sure that there's a way that they can identify the source of all these materials that have found. (personal communication, February 21, 2021)

Octavius asked Jim about his feelings toward Mimbres items in collections and exhibitions in that were possibly looted in the past. Jim answered,

Well, I think that's one of the main things that I'm really trying to make people understand and aware that just because they are Mimbres don't mean that they're not our people. Hopefully with the work that we're doing, then we can make people aware that as long as there are Puebloan people that they are our people and a lot of these sites are a clear indication of our people there at that time, and when you see all the artifacts that are [in] museums that were taken and some of them were really identified you look at the session information and museums themselves were collected, so that means it was stolen and to have that information there and if it's a really important item that we want, then we can use that just that one phrase to repatriate it back here to Zuni . . . so we might become members Salado, Hohokam all these different people are our ancestors and might be called different but for us they're still our ancestors; these Zuni people that were around within that area, so [we] want to make people aware [of] that, especially in museums. And I did a little presentation in New York Natural History and they had concretions that were considered just like marbles, and I gave him information that they're very important because if it the imports of them . . . they're found in houses . . . they're found in living areas . . . the now that they are the people that are working in the museums to get a better understanding about their handling on to have somebody telling them that it's not just a rock that was picked up off the ground; it was collected by an individual probably a medicine man that had intentions on using that specific item that was found in their houses and now there are museums that identify it as a piece of rock, but it's more important to us because of how it was collected, who collected it and what it was used for. (personal communication, February 21, 2021)

On the basis of Jim's response, Octavius further considered the importance of places that have been blessed. Jim also replied,

Right yeah, just like here in Zuni, our new home—every year for the house is blessed and these houses when they're actually built, the same principle of blessing the house was done there, and that's why you find bits of turquoise within the house in the four corners because that's how people make sure that their house was there to protect them but also to bring in with the prayers to bring in more seeds or food or children into the house, and a lot of that information has been gathered by archaeologists, but they're not aware why they are there. But this is very another important thing because turquoise in Zuni is called *X'o* and what it means, to me it's plain and the description is hard and that's what [it] means and that's what we call turquoise. It's the heart; it's what makes our people strong. It makes the house strong, so an offering left within the four corners of the house strengthens the house to protect the people in it but also to bring in all the blessings. And so, a lot of that information has not really been put out . . . especially in universities, when they do collect turquoise, they just think it was probably used as an adornment, but there's a lot of use for turquoise. And for Zuni I think the main thing is that it brings in blessings; it strengthens the house, protects the house, so why did this information has never been put out to the general public? [I] go to a lot of these museums and you see turquoise in little plastic bags, and they are identified turquoise found here and there but takes away from the importance of why the turquoise was in the house if it's not identified where it was found, so I think that's one of the things do that with archaeologists going to sites that they've clearly identify all of these little bits and pieces that were found in the house because now it will give better interpretation . . . better information to these things that are in museums and universities if they are identified where they are found. So, the setting is important to the context of the place where something was found. So if people collected in their study . . . collected some turquoise, but they're actually doing is removing what was part of the blessing of that place and removing some of the context of that blessing from that place, so these are things that's not taught in the schools and even professional archaeologists even with good intentions may think that they're collecting and keeping a record but actually what they're doing is removing some things that are intended to be there forever; not all things have to be removed. And once a place is blessed that mean they're blessed forever, right, and I think that's . . . well now we have the new educated new students that are coming out that are now using LiDAR and all these different tools that they have to identify walls and even to identify minute items that are on in the floor without going in and really digging up the site itself because there's a lot of information out there that have been produced through excavations and pretty sure what they find out with the LiDAR that they can go back to all of these reports and reference where it was found, how was found, and what the material is, and they can get a good idea of where it came from and not really destroy the site. Now we're where the Native people now are really going into not doing any excavations because it's a lot of information out there, and there was produced through a lot of excavations even here on the Zuni reservation, so it takes away from why all of these things were left behind and sometimes even taking out little things for the protection of the house might bring bad vibes omen to the people that are actually doing the excavation, and that's one thing too that has never been discussed because all these things were left behind for a reason, and if they're taken out, they're taken out of context; they are put in a situation where our ancestors might want to harm people but want to make sure that this is never done again a lot of. I know some archaeologists there . . . they think it's their knees and their hands are having problems because they've always been crawling around in science, but I'm looking at it at a different way now it's our ancestors turn to get even. (personal communication, February 21, 2021)

Both Octavius's and Jim's commentaries offer us ways non-Native archaeologists can conduct their multivocal studies with Native American elders and scholars. One lesson was the theme of collaboration. While listening to Octavius's and Jim's voices regarding their perspectives and ideas about collaborative work, it is different from how we as archaeologists generally consider an ideal collaboration. In other words, not all collaborative work between archaeologists and Native Americans is mutually beneficial, but this project taught me that such mutually beneficial collaborative work is possible.

Jim and Octavius stated that a collaborative work should create an equal balance between academics and Source Communities. Reconnecting to the ancient landscape would be one of many ways. Octavius stated during the interview that sourcing studies of turquoise allowed him to trace where these materials came from and to recognize how his ancestors traveled or had connections with those people who lived near these sourcing areas. These kinds of scientific studies would offer crucial information about the lifestyle and trade of their ancestors in the past.

Jim explicitly shared important insights into the items recovered from archaeological sites and their meaning. For example, turquoises on the four corners of an ancient room were intentionally deposited for the protection of the people, place, and environment. These leavings, according to Jim, should not be removed. Under this worldview and belief, non-Native archaeologists should be aware of and respect this kind of perspective. Importantly, when archaeologists are planning to conduct an excavation of an ancient place, we need to have clear and legitimate goals and purposes; by doing so, we must not be destroying protected lands that Source Communities want to preserve and protect for the next generations. If archaeologists cannot justify their motivations and goals, Native Americans and archaeologists cannot maintain and sustain the mutual benefit of collaborative work, and the equal balance of knowledge about the past human behaviors cannot be achieved.

Finally, Jim summarized what he thought about the landscape in Gila National Forest and its relationship to the Zunis, saying,

It's a remote area, so there's been a lot of looting. I think there is almost a fact that is, so little is known about the area relative to other parts of the Southwest makes it that much more intriguing. It makes, it's like that the hard place to do, to find some evidence, it's the hard place to do the work which makes it even more interesting to make. But I think that really like . . . just really think down, I asked we talked about five hundred years which really isn't a lot of time for Native people to be talking about. People who have moved here from Europe only three hundred or four hundred years ago, five hundred years seems like a long time, it's not much time to us. And similarly, to think about ancestral Puebloan people and Fremont people and others in Utah, people think that's so far away. How does that make any difference? Why is that so important to Zuni? It's not so far away, the Park Service used to think the Grand Canyon is so far away to Zuni, why is that important to Zuni, it's so far away? So, we think about Mimbres culture and Mimbres territory lands, people think is so far away, it's not so far away. So, I think there's more to be thought about in terms of distances in time and that movement communication, that has yet to be uncovered. So, I'm interested to see where that goes next. (personal communication, February 21, 2021)

On the basis of both Octavius's and Jim's commentaries, the most important aspect of this landscape study was that the Zuni elders could reconnect with the environment and ecology where their ancestors used to live. Although Octavius and Jim had previously come to the area for elk and wild turkey hunting, they did not know of the existence of archaeological sites there. In addition, they did not thoroughly recognize the connection between the Zuni and Mimbres peoples. Jim said, "More visiting places of my ancestors. This time in Mimbres country" (personal communication, October 22, 2019). Visiting the landscape of the Mimbres culture area allowed these elders to reconnect with their ancestors.

Both Octavius and Jim could feel strong connections with the Mimbres people. For example, when they found that a turquoise was offered to a rock art panel site, they told us that the Zunis are the only people who present turquoises as their offerings at ancient places. Therefore, their ancestors would have visited this site in the past. Octavius also mentioned that the area in Gila National Forest has been an important place for the Zunis because songbirds (swallows, swifts, etc.) migrate there. The swallows and swifts are important birds for the Zunis for their ceremonies because they metaphorically imply bringing rain/moisture. Octavius said that his ancestors knew this area and most likely came down to obtain feathers from these songbirds (Scott 2020).

The Gila National Forest is a ridged and isolated place, but both Octavius and Jim felt after this project was completed that this is still part of their ancestral lands. Without this project, these elders would not recognize and know of the existence of their ancestral land and the ancestors who inhabited this area in the past.

CONCLUSION

Since I was trained as a processual archaeologist, the landscape study with these elders opened my eyes and contradicted my perspectives regarding the frame of archaeological interpretations developed by culture history, processual archaeology, post-processual archaeology, and multivocality. By collaborating on the landscape study with the Zuni elders, I learned a great deal about how they related to the landscape in the Mimbres culture areas. Octavius and Jim generously shared their perspectives and interpretations of archaeological records, and I witnessed how Native Science could be integrated into archaeological interpretations. One of the important lessons here is that there is a lot to learn from the questions that Native Americans ask each other.

While conducting this project, I felt that I was an apprentice and acquired many lessons from these elders. For example, one of the important lessons was that by reconnecting with an ancient landscape, these Zuni elders could rewrite and redirect how their ancestors have been portrayed by ethnographers and anthropologists in the nineteenth and early twentieth centuries. This demonstrates critiques of cultural history as well as of processual archaeology paradigms in which archaeologists have used objective and systematic approaches to understand and reconstruct the relationship between humans and their environment in a particular area and have developed many geographic boundaries dividing ancient cultural groups, such as Ancestral Puebloans, Hohokam, and Mogollon cultures. However, Jim and Octavius stressed that their ancestors frequently moved around, married in and out, and traveled many places to procure natural resources and to meet other people. Octavius strongly emphasized that archaeologists have segregated ancient people into many different groups in prehistory, but Pueblo people share a similar origin.

Landscape studies in archaeology is one of the abstract topics for which it is difficult to tease out how ancient people utilized and conceived a particular land. However, listening to and integrating Native Science helps us deepen our understanding of landscapes. As this project demonstrates, Source Communities like the Zuni elders can offer us alternative descriptions and interpretations to compare with archaeologists' interpretations of the landscape. For example, while listening to the Zuni elders' narratives regarding the cultural landscape in Gila National Forest, I recognized that they are connected to their ancestors who lived in the landscape a long time ago. In addition, their perspectives regarding the landscape are deeply allied with the life of continuum sequence. These perspectives are immensely different from how archaeologists see landscapes as locations filled with tangible evidence that Western archaeologists use to define cultural groups.

Drawing on the themes emerged from observing Native Science at work, in the next chapter, I will continue discussing how the different archaeological methodologies interact by introducing correlative archaeology.

1. Jim Enote and Octavius Seowtewa prefer to use the term "Indigenous ways of knowing" instead of "Native Science." However, the first author considers that both Indigenous ways of knowing and Native Science have similar concepts and definitions. Thus, in the majority of discussions in this chapter as well as other chapters, the term "Native Science" is used.

2. https://anthropology.nmsu.edu/anthropology-faculty/f-arakawa.html

Chapter 7

Correlative Archaeology

Readers might wonder why I am waiting until the end to talk about the main theme of the book, "correlative archaeology" (also "correlative thinking"). In doing this, I am following a traditional Japanese (or Asian) writing style that makes the conclusion the climax of subject matter. In Chinese/Japanese poetry, the writing system consists of the four-part structure "起承転結" (*ki-shou-ten-ketsu* in Japanese), which means "introduction-development-turn (or twist)-conclusion." This writing structure is valued in Japan (and China as well as Korea). In contrast to the thesis-evidence-conclusion structure in Western argumentative writing, the Asian writing style is a way to avoid declaring an absolute statement or truth; many Asians believe that a conclusive statement or truth based on observation, experiment, and/or experience has both pros and cons, and it cannot be absolutely true.

I believe that this epistemic value might be derived from a Buddhist ontology which emphasizes impermanence, nothingness, or non-attachment, as I discussed in the preface. The writing style of this book can be applied to the four-part structure: the preface and the introduction are the "introduction"; the discussion of culture history (Chapter 2), processual archaeology (Chapter 3), and post-processual archaeology (Chapter 4) are the "development"; multivocality (Chapter 5) and Native Science (Chapter 6) are the "turn or twist"; and correlative archaeology (Chapter 7) is the "conclusion." This writing structure is integral to the argument of the book because it allows me to situate the embodied and intellectual dimensions of my research, recognize the contributions and limitations of different archaeological methodologies, contribute new data to the conversation, and now offer a theory or correlative archaeology as a practice of embracing and relating multiple truths.

As I discussed in the preface, my positionality as an archaeologist is unique. I am a Japanese foreign national, trained in processual archaeology here in the United States, studying archaeological remains related to Native Americans in the American Southwest. This is not to say that other archaeologists do not also bring a unique perspective to their interpretations (they do), but to point out that my upbringing in Japan and my experiences here in the United States as a Japanese foreign national have a profound effect on the way I see and relate to objects and people. In other words, one of the goals of this book is to consider how my Asian identity, vocational training, and relationship to the subject matter correlates in my interpretations of artifacts and landscapes.

I would also like to think that my doing this is not seen as solipsistic. Instead, I hope that this book invites archaeologists who come from different backgrounds and study artifacts of different cultures in other places the opportunity to reflect more on how their positionality shapes their interpretations in ways that might not yet be accounted for. Surely, archaeology as a field can benefit more from this type of reflection, and I would hope that correlative archaeology would provide a possible methodology.

For those who are not familiar with correlative thinking, it can be understood as an associated relationship or a connection between two or more things. For example, my background as a Japanese archaeologist who is trained in Western methodologies and studying Native American artifacts can be understood as promoting correlative thinking. And to be sure, my Japanese worldview is an impetus to correlate meaning by challenging, questioning, and expanding archaeological interpretations. For example, while I am trained in processual archaeology, I often find myself trying to understand how Native Americans might have experienced or thought about the objects that I am studying. In this capacity, correlative thinking enables me to examine the practice of archaeological interpretation in a way that accounts for my different commitments and my Asian worldviews.

Digging a little deeper, the origin of correlative thinking can be found in classical Chinese cosmologies (e.g., the *Book of Changes/Transformation* or *I Ching*, Taoism, and/or the Yin-Yang school). Hall and Ames (1998) defined correlative thinking as a "species of analogy" and further stated, "Correlative thinking is a species of spontaneous thinking grounded in informal and ad hoc analogical procedures presupposing both association and differentiation" (1998, 1). In other words, through correlative thinking, people can create meaning by making connections. For example, the season "spring" can be connected to the direction of east, the color of green, the climatic condition of wind, or the liver which regulates the body's nourishments, and those who have experienced a spring after a cold winter might feel optimistic and recognize it as a time of beginning. It is in these associative capacities where correlative thinking differs from the analytical or causal thinking (Western philosophies), which, following our example, might instead try to define spring, understand its causes and effects, or compare it to other seasons. This is not to say that correlative thinking is irrational or defies logic—it is both rational and logical. Correlative thinking just moves differently as a faculty of reason; whereas analytical thinking is linear, correlative thinking is circular. In this regard, one might think of correlative thinking as the counterpart to analytical thinking—or the yin to the yang of correlative thinking, if you prefer.

To understand this better, perhaps it is worth looking at the English and Japanese (or its close relative, Chinese) languages as vehicles of thought or syntagms (Graham 1989). For example, in the English sentence "The sun is bright," meaning relies on the agreement between noun, verb, and adjective. In contrast, meaning in Japanese/Chinese ideograms is grounded in correlative thinking that induces meaning-making by association between juxtaposed images and their related concepts. For example, in Japanese, *mei* 明 (日 sun plus 月 moon creates 明 light/bright) plus *hi/nichi* 日 (sun/sun goddess in Shintoism) creates 明日 (tomorrow). What is important to note here is that the correlative meaning has an existential dimension to it: One can see the sun reflecting the moon and see that it is bright with one's own eyes, just as one might relate to sun/sun goddess and thus tomorrow as something hopeful and bright. In this sense, meaning in Chinese characters is conveyed through pictographs that are at least in part rooted in the visual representation of ideas. To be sure, this kind of meaning-making does share commonality with what we understand as poetics in the West, but instead of being seen as a form of art, correlative thinking is the root of meaning-making in East Asian thought.

Beyond poetics, what is most compelling about correlative thinking is that it offers us a structural framework to create connections and relationships between seemingly unrelated things and/or among yet unexplored relationships. Or, as Graham (1989, 321) says, "When the pattern is familiar this is no more than the recurrence of habitual expectation, when a new pattern takes shape, it is sudden insight. . . . The expectations spring from and are initially confirmed by experience." In other words, correlative thinking is a way to create meaning from experience. Further, he says, "You can criticize correlations, but you cannot dispense with them" (1989, 323). This is just a reminder that while any interpretation might be criticized, you cannot simply dismiss them or put them over "there." There is a relationship, and we are best served by trying to understand that relationship even if it is not readily intelligible to us.

Unlike analytical thinking, correlative thinking focuses on movement and transformation that occurs from different types of interactions. This structural approach to correlative thinking is most easily demonstrated in looking at the five elements that are derived from the classical Chinese text the *I Ching* (Govinda 1981), or the *Book of Transformations*, which was written about 5,000 years ago. The *I Ching* consists of eight trigrams (or bagua) that symbolize the interplay of Yin-Yang (yin—negative, dark, and feminine;

yang—positive, bright, and masculine). Wilhelm et al. (1950, 1), one of the early translators of the *I Ching*, offers the following understanding of the trigrams:

> The eight trigrams are symbols standing for changing transitional states; they are the images that are constantly undergoing change. Attention centers not on things in their state of being . . . but upon their movements in change. The eight trigrams therefore are not representative of things as such but of their tendencies in movement. . . . Further, they represented a family consisting of a father, mother, three sons, and three daughters . . . in what might be called an abstract sense.

Of the eight, the Heaven (天) and Earth (地) trigrams can be thought of as the creative and receptive forces or "father" and "mother," and the Thunder (雷) trigram as the "inciting" or "first son" (Wilhelm et al. 1950). Heaven is the spiritual or formless, Earth is the material or formed, and Thunder is the "arousing principle" (Govinda 1981, 16). The Wuxing (five elements) are derived from the trigrams Lake (湖), Fire (火), Wind/Wood (風/木), Water (水), and Mountain (山) and referred to as Metal, Water, Wood, Fire, and Earth in their elemental application.

In looking at the eight trigrams as a whole, one of the most important insights into Taoist philosophy is in how they arranged the eight trigrams (bagua) both abstractly and temporally; whereas one system (Fu Hi) focused on the polarity or opposites, the other (King Wen) focused on the sequential and experienced (Govinda 1981). Albeit, in different ways, the Taoist also saw the possibility of different arrangements in five elements—namely in the generative, destructive, and demeaning cycles. As I will discuss more fully in the next section, it is important to understand each element both abstractly as a correlative symbol with multiple associations and temporally as an element in relation to the other elements. In regard to the capacity for elements to relate to one another, I will refer to these movement-oriented relationships as cycles. In looking at the correspondences or associative faculties of elements, I will focus on each element's ability to be applied to different contexts under investigation.

ELEMENTS AS ASSOCIATIVE SYMBOLS

Correlative thinking can perhaps be best understood by examining how the Taoist associated each element to different types of manifestations that humans experienced in place, body, or thought. In this capacity, each element corresponds to physical (e.g., organs, directions, planets, seasons), sensual (e.g., feelings, tastes, colors, sounds), and conceptual (e.g., virtues, actions) phenomena (see Table 1.1). By looking at each element on its own, we are able to, for example, correlate fire with the direction of the south, the season of summer, the condition of rising, the process of growth, the feeling of happiness, the color of red, and the heart and small intestine in the human body. Importantly, and as I will try to demonstrate momentarily, it is in each element's capacity to correspond to different subjects of investigation that I am able to develop a theory of correlative archaeology that corresponds to the physical, sensual, and conceptual dimension of different archaeological methodologies. Before we do that work, however, it is important to examine how the Taoist understood the relationships between the elements as movements of cycles.

THE FIVE ELEMENTS AS CYCLES

The five elements present us with an opportunity to develop a structural model of correlative thinking by examining the possibilities of movement. When articulating the relationships between Metal, Water, Earth, Fire, and Wood, the Taoist identified three different cycles: 1) generative, 2)

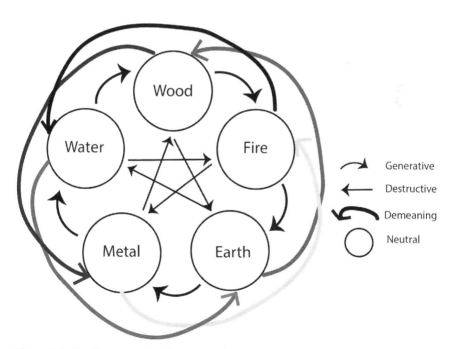

Figure 7.1. Five Elements, showing generative, destructive, and demeaning cycles.

destructive, and 3) demeaning (Figure 7.1). The generative cycle can be understood as one element producing another. In the generative cycle, metal produces water, water nourishes wood, wood feeds fire, fire produces earth, and earth generates metal. The destructive cycle is understood as one element countering another: fire melts metal, metal cuts wood, wood weakens earth, earth absorbs water, and water extinguishes fire. The demeaning cycle is understood as one element insulting or diminishing another: wood dulls metal, metal pokes fire, fire agitates water, water destabilizes earth, and earth rots wood.

Altogether, what is compelling about the five elements is that the Taoist were able to correlate the different elements to different types of physical, sensual, and conceptual phenomenon and then apply cycles to understand how different things related to one another through processes of becoming and transformation. For example, the Taoist applied the five elements to develop a theory and practice for music, martial arts, culinary arts, medicine, psychology, agriculture, astronomy, and so on. It is in this capacity that I propose to apply the five elements to archaeology. In order to make connections to correlative thinking and to recognize my work as an academic exercise, rather than a Taoist practice, I will use the term correlative archaeology.

Archaeological Methods as Associative Practices

Just as the Taoist understood each element to have its physical, sensual, and conceptual qualities, archaeologists recognize that all methodologies have their ontological commitments, epistemic virtues, and conceptual application that enable them to develop research questions, design a methodology, and make contributions to the field's body of knowledge. It is also in this capacity that I propose to associate the different methodologies covered in this book (i.e., culture history, processual, post-processual, multivocality, and Native Science) to their respective ontological commitments, epistemic virtues, and conceptual application.

I recognize that these terms are somewhat ambiguous and arbitrary, but for the purposes of making my argument, I define ontological commitments as the way in which the methodology shapes or limits the questions an archaeologist asks about what an artifact is; epistemic virtues as values that a practitioner of a particular methodology adheres to in the production of knowledge; and conceptual application as the manner in which a researcher contributes to the conversation (see Table 7.1). Of course, we could further break down the associative qualities of any given methodology by, for example, identifying tools, coding practices, or discursive heuristics, but for the sake of simplicity I will focus on ontological commitments, epistemic virtues, and conceptual

Table 7.1. An example of the associative dimensions of the elements as relationships to apparitions in the world.

Methodology	Ontological Commitments (i.e., questions a methodology might ask)	Epistemic Virtues (i.e., the values a methodology might hold to in answering the question)	Conceptual Application (i.e., how the production of knowledge is used)
Culture History	To what cultural group does an artifact belong?	The artifacts are evidence that the culture lived in a place and time.	To map out and define ancient cultures in time and place.
Processual	How was this artifact used by a culture?	The artifacts are evidence of a social and economic structure.	To understand the cause and effect of ancient social and economic structures.
Post-Processual	How was this artifact used by an individual? How are our biases shaping our research?	The artifacts are evidence of individual agency in a culture. Our interpretations are evidence of our bias.	To understand the power dynamics and agency of ancient cultures and peoples. To reflect on and critique our biases.
Multivocality	How do Native people understand the artifact?	The artifacts are multifaceted and complex.	To decolonialize archaeological practices and to socially construct knowledge.
Native Science	How do we [Indigenous people] relate to the artifact?	The artifacts are evidence of our [Indigenous people's] ancestors and meaningful to us.	To relate to our [Indigenous people's] ancestors and educate future generations. To recognize the embodied and existential dimensions of meaning-making.

application as overarching categories from which one could further extrapolate if desired.

To be sure, albeit in different terms at times, these are the kinds of questions, practices, and applications that I have tried to demonstrate in each of the respective chapters in this book. For example, in Chapter 5, I tried to show how multivocality treats Mimbres pottery and designs as complex and multifaceted artifacts that are understood by Native peoples in different ways. Further, Chapter 5 was also an effort to decolonize the interpretations proposed by archaeologists who practiced culture history (Chapter 2), processual (Chapter 3), and/or post-processual (Chapter 4) methodologies. And in Chapter 6, I tried to show how Native Science or Indigenous ways of knowing can open the conversation up (i.e., beyond the often narrow and limited concerns of archaeologists) and allow archaeologists to understand artifacts in different ways and contexts. Further, Chapter 6 was also an effort to remind archaeologists that the artifacts have value and meaning that are not only outside of academic concerns but also inaccessible to us (non-Native archaeologists) in practice. In the next section, I will demonstrate how we can take correlative archaeology a step further by turning our attention to the cyclical application of the five elements.

Archaeological Methods as Cycles

Unlike the periodic table of elements, which lineates elements according to mass and taxonomic group, Taoist understood elements as transformative symbols where one element generates, destroys, or weakens another in predictable patterns that depend on the circumstance of their interaction; while water might put out a fire if poured over it (destructive cycle), fire might agitate or evaporate water if placed under it (demeaning cycle). From a discursive point of view, the different archaeological methodologies interact

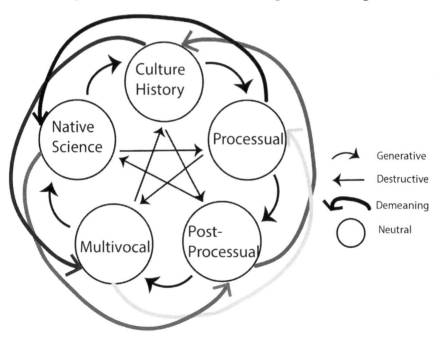

Figure 7.2. The Conceptualized Three Different Cycles in Archaeological Interpretations, Using the Five Element Cycles.

in similarly generative, destructive, and demeaning ways (Figure 7.2). In organizing this book, for example, I tried to demonstrate how culture history produced a body of knowledge that made the processual methodologies possible. Without having defined cultural groups, processual archaeologists would have a hard time knowing who's economic or social structures they are trying to understand. Just as without a structural understanding of these cultural groups, post-processual critiques and concerns would not exist. One can also see that if it were not for critiques of archaeology as a colonial practice, multivocality would not be practiced. Recognizing the agency of Indigenous peoples, multivocality becomes an opportunity for Native Scientists to generate their own questions and concerns about the artifacts. And was it not Indigenous ways of knowing that generated the artifacts to be investigated in the first place?

Drawing on the destructive and demeaning cycles, one can easily enough correlate similar types of relationships between the methodologies. For example, as authorities Native Science destroys the speculation and hypothesis of processual archaeologists, but at the same time the exacting tools and empirical methodologies of processual archaeologists demean the oral traditions and embodied perceptions of Native Scientists. Of course, discursive practices and methodologies are messy, mixed, and complex, and it would be misleading or at least contrived to limit the way one methodology relates to another through strict structural artifice. However, my hope is that one can see how it is possible to correlate different types of insights by extrapolating from notions of the generative, destructive, and demeaning cycles. In order to demonstrate how correlative archaeology might be applied, in the next section I draw on findings and discussions from Chapters 2 through 6 to provide a few examples.

CORRELATIVE ARCHEOLOGY APPLIED

In order to demonstrate how one might apply correlative thinking to archaeology as a tool of analysis and meaning-making, in this section I will correlate the findings of the case studies in Chapters 5 (Hopi artists) and 6 (Zuni elders) to one another and to Chapters 2 (culture history), 3 (processual), and 4 (post-processual). I use Chapters 5 and 6 as the point of reference because they are the chapters in which I conducted primary research as an archaeologist for this book. In other words, whereas Chapters 2 through 4 were more along the lines of a literature review to help me situate and develop a theory for correlative archaeology, in Chapters 5 and 6 I was practicing and presenting data from the multivocal and Native Science methodologies.

Here I should also note that it is not realistically possible to practice correlative archaeology as a primary researcher in every methodology nor is this something I am trying to advocate for. In the applied sense, I propose correlative archaeology as a method to help archaeologists correlate the primary research they have produced (from any given methodologies) to the findings of existent research (produced by researchers from other methodologies) or to correlate existing data as a secondary researcher in new ways.

Further, as I have tried to demonstrate in this book, it is important to recognize that archaeological methodologies are discursive practices that develop in response to historical contexts, bodies, questions, criticisms, technological advances, and other productions of knowledge in complex ways. Just as the Taoist understood elements as processes of becoming in complex ways, all methodologies are interconnected in their process of becoming. The point being that correlative thinking offers us the opportunity to examine connections proximately (i.e., one methodology in relation to another within a particular cycle) and holistically (i.e., all methodologies in relation). To demonstrate this, I will apply the three cycles to demonstrate different types of correlative thinking between methodologies and speak to the bigger picture of the methodologies in relation.

Generative Correlations

In generative correlations, the term "informing" expresses the relationship between different methodologies. One methodology informs another: culture history informs processual archaeology; processual archaeology informs post-processual archaeology; post-processual archaeology informs multivocality; multivocality informs Native Science; and Native Science informs culture history. I demonstrated the generative cycle of archaeological interpretations using the Mimbres culture as a case study from Chapter 2 to Chapter 6 where each methodology, in certain capacities, informs the next in a generative manner. To consider how particular generative correlations work, I turn our attention to the informing relationships between post-processualism and multivocality and then multivocality and Native Science.

In Chapter 4, we examined how post-processualism allowed archaeologists to reflect on their biases and ask questions about artifacts that recognized the agency of individuals in ancient cultures. In this capacity, one of the challenges that post-processual archaeologists faced was how archaeologists could methodologically produce knowledge outside of their gaze and respect the agency of individuals who no longer remain. In Chapter 5, we looked at how multivocality, in part, developed in response to these disciplinary challenges. By incorporating the voices of descendant groups, archaeologists were at once able to consider opinions and evidence outside of their purview and to honor the agency of Indigenous peoples. Artifacts, in this capacity, became subjects of discussion between archaeologists and Native people. In my particular experience, I was trained as a processual archaeologist and if it were not for the concerns that post-processualism made me aware of, I would not have had the wherewithal or understood the need to collaborate with the Hopi artists. It was in this capacity that post-processualism informed my decision to design and participate in a multivocal study.

The informative relationship between multivocality and Native Science allows us to consider generative correlations in similar but also different capacities. If one recognizes that the conceptual movement or tendency of post-processualism is to reflect and critique, it is easy enough to see how post-processualism also generated Native Science in the sense that as long as there was an archaeologist mediating the conversation, the biases of the researcher were always present, and the agency of Native peoples could not be fully recognized. In a more existential capacity, my wanting to learn more from Native Scientists about the Mimbres landscape emerged from my participation in the multivocal study with the Hopi artists; it was through my conversations with them that I realized that there was a lot I didn't know and/ or couldn't relate to as a processuralist (or post-processualist, if that is what I had become).

Here I should also remind the reader that many of the most important insights generated from the Native Science research occurred when I stepped back and listened to the Zuni elders ask each other questions—in part because they didn't think that I did a good job of asking questions. Again, here one might also say that post-processualism informed me in the sense that it made me aware of issues related to power dynamics and agency as a researcher. It is also important to note that just as the Taoist understood that metal produces water—produces wood—produces fire (and so on) in an interconnected process of becoming, insights from generative correlations in archeology are not restricted to the methodology that might seem to immediately proceed or follow.

Destructive Correlations

Destructive correlations can be understood by the term "contradiction." If the evidence or conclusions produced by one methodology contradict the findings of another methodology in a manner that does not inform (i.e., generate) new insights or provoke (i.e., demean) new questions, it can be understood as destructive correlation. In instances such as this, the truth or data of one methodology overcomes the truth or data of another methodology: culture history contradicts post-processual; post-processual contradicts Native Science; Native Science contradicts processual archaeology; processual archaeology contradicts multivocality; and multivocality contradicts culture history. To demonstrate how destructive correlations might be recognized and applied, I turn our attention to the destructive relationships between multivocality and culture history and between post-processual and Native Science.

In Chapter 2, I introduced the culture history paradigm as a framework that enabled early American archaeologists to map and define ancient cultures in time and space by coding artifacts according to cultural groups and their artistic and technological developments. In the Southwest of the United States, this enabled archaeologists to reify terms like Mimbres as a distinct cultural group that lived in southern New Mexico, southeastern Arizona, and northern Mexico from AD 900 to 1130. In Chapter 5, I presented the multivocal paradigm as a framework that created opportunities for archaeologists to listen to descendant groups. In listening to the Hopi artists' understandings of their ancestors, it became clear that culture history terms, such as Ancestral Pueblo, Hohokam, and Mogollon, were arbitrary and static understandings for them, if not inaccurate. The Hopi artists believed that their ancestral groups migrated in and out frequently for a long period of time. Therefore, looking at a Mimbres bowl design, we should consider the multiple origins of Pueblo groups who manufactured and used it. In this capacity, the knowledge produced by the multivocal paradigm contradicts the knowledge produced by the culture history paradigm in ways that can't be reconciled or confirmed by culture historians.

By turning our attention to the relationship between the post-processual methodology covered in Chapter 4 and the Native Science paradigm covered in Chapter 6, another capacity of destructive correlations emerges. One of the tenets of post-processualism is that knowledge should be democratic or decentralized. While this epistemic value was developed in critique of the authority assumed by archaeologists, the critical direction or tendency of movement associated with post-processualism still allows us to bring into question the authority of Native Scientists who might otherwise go unchecked because Native Scientists are operating a place of epistemic embodiment that is inaccessible to non-Native scholars. Whereby, for example, post-processualism might not be able to contradict the interpretations of the Zuni elders, post-processualism can, for example, remind us of the gender biases that might be present in the Zuni elders' insights or argue for the need to supplement the insights from the Zuni elders by being more inclusive and diversifying participants (e.g., Acoma, Laguna, and other pueblo groups) in Native Science studies. In other words, by focusing on the ontological and epistemic behaviors of different methodologies, destructive correlations might offer us some interesting insights into a relationship that might otherwise seem non-essential or at least unarticulated.

Demeaning Correlations

One of the interesting qualities of demeaning correlations is that they provide an opportunity for a methodology to counter the paradigm that destroys or contradicts it by, for example, invoking a rebuttal or citing evidence that its destroyer fails to account for. In this capacity, demeaning correlations can best be understood by the idea of a counterargument or question that might expose the parochial concerns of a methodology as a structural limitation and/or bring into question the ethical underpinnings of a methodology as an innate flaw. Structurally speaking, the demeaning correlation is a direct response to the destructive relationship: culture history questions multivocality; multivocality questions processual archaeology; processual archaeology questions Native Science; Native Science questions post-processual archaeology; and post-processual archaeology questions culture history. To demonstrate how demeaning correlations might help archaeologists, I turn our attention to the demeaning relationships between culture history and multivocality and between Native Science and post-processual.

In the destructive correlations, we looked at how the Hopi artists' understanding of their ancestral history contradicted the terminology created by culture historians. While culture historians might not have evidence or the ethical grounds to invalidate Indigenous ways of knowing, they can still defend their claims or point to flaws in multivocal research. For example, culture historians might ask the Hopi artists, "If our terminologies are incorrect, to whom should we attribute the accumulation of artifacts that were only found in this specific region?" Or, in a similar manner, culture historians might contend that "if we need to account for many migrations over long periods of time, and since the method for making Mimbres painted pottery consists of sand temper, kaolin clay for slip, and mineral paint that the Hopi did not use, then maybe we need to question the authority of a particular descendant group."

In returning to the relationship between post-processualism and Native Science, whereas in the destructive correlation post-processualism contradicted Indigenous ways of knowing, in the demeaning correlation we consider the possible counters and questions of Native Science. For starters, if non-Native post-processual archaeologists were trying to undermine the authority of the Zuni elders on the grounds of not being democratic or having gender biases, the Zuni elders would only need to point to the hypocritical nature of the allegations by pointing to how post-processualists were still imposing their democratic values and cultural worldviews on Native peoples under the umbrella of a colonial legacy that archaeologists cannot get out from under.

Complex Correlations

If the above, albeit contrived and speculative at times, allows us to examine particular types of correlations that help us understand, examine, and cross-examine data in different ways, it would be an oversight to end this section before reminding the reader that correlations should not be reduced to linear, structural, or direct applications. More than anything else, I would like to leave the reader with the idea of correlations as tendencies of movement in thought. In this capacity, one might think of culture history as the tendency to define, processualism as the tendency to understand cause and effect, post-processualism as the tendency to reflect and critique, multivocality as the tendency to understand knowledge as social constructions, and Native Science as the tendency to recognize the embodied and existential dimension of knowledge. With these different types of movements in mind, archaeologists might be able to better articulate their limitations, recognize their biases, or point to areas where there is a need for more research.

LIMITATIONS AND FUTURE CORRELATIONS

Drawing on the Taoist philosophy of the five elements, in this chapter I developed and applied a methodology of correlative archaeology that allowed me to generate, contradict, and question primary data from multivocal and Native Science with secondary research from culture history, processualism, and post-processualism. The goal of this work was to at once 1) articulate the ontological and epistemic underpinnings of each methodology so that we can better see how each methodology contributes to and limits our interpretation of an artifact; 2) bring the different methodologies into conversation with one another in structural ways (i.e., through the generative, destructive, and demeaning cycles) that reveal different types of insights; and 3) to account for my personal ontological assumptions and epistemological commitments as a researcher from the Far East.

From another vantage point, one might also describe the function of this work to be putting Western, Native American, and East Asian worldviews into conversation with one another in an effort to mediate or get outside of what is often reduced to an Indigenous-colonial binary. Altogether, it was an interesting if not productive exercise of transposing East Asian philosophy to my concerns as a Western archaeologist working in collaboration with Native American artists and scientists. Of course, a project such as this has its share of limitations and beyond a curiosity; it is obvious that one cannot say, "I will use correlative archaeology to tackle unresolved archaeological questions," but my hope is that what I have sought to accomplish in this book might be of value to archaeologists and scholars regardless of their research interests and personal background.

In writing this book and developing a theory of correlative archaeology, I was always aware of two obstacles that might bring into question the usefulness and limits of my work: the structural constraints of the theory and the fact that I am Japanese. Spoken from a doubtful and skeptical second person, the structural concerns go something like this: *You arbitrarily choose five methodologies to align with the five elements; surely there are more than five methodologies and/or what if there were less? Further, while structure is nice and neat, discourse is far more complicated than three types of possible interactions.* To be sure, these are objective and personal concerns of my own, and the only way that I can answer them is by drawing on Eastern philosophy.

First off, one of the traps that both the Taoist and Buddhist sought to avoid was in naming or limiting concepts or being to names or fixed understandings. Of course, in conceptualizing the theory of the five elements, the Taoist were not trying to reduce our physical, sensual, and conceptual experience to five things. Again, and drawing on Wilhelm et al.'s (1950, 1) articulation of the eight trigrams of the *I Ching*, which are not things but "symbols standing for changing transitional states," the elements are not things but symbols for transmutable states. In this capacity, I would argue the methodologies are also not things but symbols for transmutable states. I mean this in several ways; first to remind us that culture history, processualism, post-processualism, multivocality, and Indigenous ways of knowing are not singular to archaeology. Just like correlative thinking was adapted from Taoist philosophy, each of the methodologies discussed in this book is derived from other theories and adapted to the purposes of archaeology. For example, processualism has its roots in positivism, which can be traced back to ancient Greece, whose philosophers surely were not thinking about archaeologists studying Mimbres' pottery in the United States.

Further, and following, it is important to remember that none of the methodologies covered in this book are fixed practices. For example, as new technologies develop so too will the methodological practice of processualism, and as new critical-cultural theories develop so too will the concerns of post-processualism. In other words, just as elements have characteristics and tendencies of movement, so do methodologies (i.e., paradigms shape questions and answers). Further, the work of correlating a methodology to an "element" would be just that—to focus on ontological and epistemic tendencies, all of which can be traced back to their roots.

In regard to correlating fewer methodologies, one only need to be reminded that the elements themselves are derived from a correlative binary of Yin-Yang or that the Heaven, Earth, and Thunder trigrams form a correlative triad, which is to remind us that from the beginning the Taoist operated in

collapsible and expandable scales of correlative thought. What is most important in correlative thinking, regardless of the scale or structure, is that the possibility of relationships presents us with an opportunity to facilitate different
kinds of conversations, be that generatively, destructively, or demeaningly.
Of course, just as medicine or science is practiced differently by different
people, how we understand or articulate the meaning of those relationships is
ultimately a limitation of our ability as embodied thinkers and by no means a
"structural flaw." Further, if three cycles feel too reductive or do not offer a
complete picture, it is by no means wrong to correlate in all possible relations
(and to be sure, even though I did not cover them in this book, there are two
more cycles within the five elements, for five in total, that together account
for all of the permutations).

In regard to my being Japanese and developing a theory that derives from
my cultural background and disposition, readers might wonder whether correlative archaeology (drawing on Buddhist and Taoist philosophies) can only
be used by East Asian people or those who practice Eastern philosophies.
If readers feel this way, it is not my intention, but I recognize the concerns.
One of the implicit arguments I have made in this book is that Indigenous
peoples have sciences and ways of knowing that are uniquely derived from
their cultural background. Similarly, at times, I have reminded readers that
to be a practicing archaeologist in the United States, one must be trained and
vetted by Western institutions which have their own mechanisms of inclusion
and exclusion. Further, I spent a considerable amount of time discussing my
cultural background to account for my bias and to situate the cultural underpinnings of correlative thinking. Point being that ethos already has a cultural,
embodied, and material dimension to it, and it would be inconsistent for me to
say that all can practice and access East Asian philosophies in the same way.

However, one must also remember that I am trained in the values and ethics of Western archaeology, and in this capacity, one of my goals in writing
this book was to contribute to the discourse in ways that others might be
able to follow for their own purposes and intents regardless of their cultural
background. It is for this reason that I have developed this book around the
Western terminology of correlative thinking, rather than Taoist or Buddhist
thinking, so that readers might focus on the idea and be more receptive to the
possibility of future applications rather than getting caught up in the cultural
context. This is not to say that the cultural context does not matter, but to
argue for a way of thinking that has application beyond a point of origin. Just
as correlative thinking is something that can be done by anyone, I offer *correlative archaeology* as a conceptual framework to anyone who might find
it useful.

In the big picture, not only is correlative thinking a useful structural
framework for archaeological interpretations, but it can also apply to other

disciplines, such as rhetoric, history, sociology, and psychology, among many others. In short, any discipline that utilizes different and sometimes competing methodologies to conduct primary research can apply correlative thinking to create conversations between the different methodologies as demonstrated in this chapter. For other archaeologists, I hope that the content and context of this book allows archaeologists who come from different backgrounds and study artifacts of different cultures in other places to reflect more on how their positionality might shape their interpretations in ways that might not yet be integrated. I hope that archaeologists can benefit more from this type of positionality and reflection in the development of archaeological methods and theories. Overall, correlative archaeology is applicable for high-level and big questions, such as the development of archaeological theories and methods. The author hopes that American archaeologists will consider correlative archaeology (or thinking) and apply for diverse interpretations pertaining to abstract signs embedded in prehistoric objects and spaces in archaeological records.

CONCLUDING REMARKS

With many Buddhas in mind, in this book I considered the many interpretations of Mimbres pottery. Through culture history, I was able to map and document the artifacts of Mimbres culture in time and space. Through processualism, I was able to understand Mimbres pottery as evidence of a complex social and economic structure. Post-processualism allowed me to criticize the colonial gaze of my understanding and ask questions about the agency of individuals as embodied empowered people. Multivocality brought Native voices and insights into the conversation, allowing me to culturally situate designs, tools, materials, and context for use and importantly to ponder the affective and spiritual dimensions of the artist-mind's eye. Native Science allowed me to experience the land and consider questions in ways beyond my purview.

My purview, of course, is rooted in my vocational training as a Western archaeologist and my cultural upbringing in Japan. If the former taught me truth through science and empirical methodology, the latter taught me to recognize impermanence, nothingness, and many truths. To be sure, the five chapters that precede this conclusion are an effort to practice archaeology as a science; just as the preface, introduction, and work here in this conclusion are an effort to not only acknowledge and account for my cultural upbringing but to make a science of it. To do this work, in this chapter I proposed and developed a theory for correlative archaeology that draws on Taoist philosophy.

Altogether, this book might remind some of the Buddhist parable about the blind men and the elephant: Hearing an unfamiliar animal, each blind man approaches the elephant and begins to describe it by that part that they touch or the limits of their experience—a tusk, a tail, an ear, a leg, or a broadside. Depending on how the parable is told, the blind men either begin to fight with one another about the truth of their experience, converse with one another to describe the elephant as a whole, or listen to one another and recognize the limits of their interpretation. And perhaps it best to end here, to offer correlative archaeology as a method to do all of these things.

References

Anschuetz, Kurt. 2005. "Landscapes as Memory: Archaeological History to Learn From and to Live By." In *Engaged Anthropology: Research Essays on North American Archaeology, Ethnobotany, and Museology*, edited by Michelle B. Hegmon, Sunday Eiselt, and Richard I. Ford, 52–72. Ann Arbor: University of Michigan, Museum of Anthropology.

Anschuetz, Kurt. 2006. "An Archaeology of Footprints: The Becoming of the Tewa Cultural Community." *Newsletter of the New Mexico Archeological Council.* Albuquerque, New Mexico.

Anschuetz, Kurt, Richard H. Wilshusen, and Cherie L. Scheick. 2010. "An Archaeology of Landscapes: Perspectives and Directions." *Journal of Archaeological Research* 9, no. 2: 157–211.

Anyon, Roger, and T. J. Ferguson. 1995. "Cultural Resources Management at the Pueblo of Zuni, New Mexico, USA." *Antiquity* 69, no. 266: 913–30.

Anyon, Roger, T. J. Ferguson, Loretta Jackson, Lillie Lane, and Phillip Vicenti. 1997. "Native American Oral Tradition and Archaeology Issues of Structure Relevance, and Respect." In *Native Americans and Archaeologists: Stepping Stones to Common Ground*, edited by Nina Swidler, Kurt E. Dongoske, Roger Anyon, and Alan S. Downer, 77–87. Walnut Creek, CA: AltaMira Press.

Anyon, Roger, Patricia A. Gilman, and Steven A. LeBlanc. 1981. "A Re-evaluation of the Mogollon-Mimbres Archaeological Sequence." *Kiva* 46: 209–25.

Arakawa, Fumiyasu. 2013. "Lithics and Male & Female Activity Spheres in the Agricultural Society of the Central Mesa Verde Region, American Southwest." *Kiva* 78: 279–312.

Arakawa, Fumiyasu, and Atsunori Ito. 2019. Living in Sacred Continuum. Las Cruces, New Mexico, University Museum, April 26, 2019.

Atalay, Sonya. 2006. "Indigenous Archaeology as Decolonizing Practice." *American Indian Quarterly* 30, no. 3: 280–310.

Atalay, Sonya. 2008. "Multivocality and Indigenous Archaeologies." In *Evaluating Multiple Narratives: Beyond Nationalist, Colonialist, and Imperialist Archaeologies*, edited by Junko Habu, Clare Fawcett, and John Matsunaga, 29–44. New York: Springer Press.

Atalay, Sonya. 2012. *Community-Based Archaeology: Research with, by and for Indigenous and Local Communities*. Berkeley: University of California Press.

Barber, Elizabeth W. 1994. *Women's Work: The First 10,000 Years*. New York: W. W. Norton.

Belknap, Bill, and Fred Kabotie. 1977. *Fred Kabotie: Hopi Indian Artist: An Autobiography Told with Bill Belknap*. Flagstaff: Museum of Northern Arizona.

Berlant, Tony. 1983. "Mimbres Painting: An Artist's Perspective." In *Mimbres Pottery: Ancient Art of the American Southwest*, edited by J. J. Brody, Catherine J. Scott, and Steven A. LeBlanc, 69–127. New York: Hudson Hills Press.

Berlant, Tony, and Evan Maurer. 2017. *Decoding Mimbres Painting: Ancient Ceramics of the American Southwest*. New York: DelMonico Books.

Bernardini, Wesley, Stewart B. Koyiyumptewa, Gregson Schachner, and Leigh Kuwanwisiwma. 2021. *Becoming Hopi: A History*. Tucson: University of Arizona Press.

Bertelsen, Raidar, Arnvid Lillehammer, and Jenny-Rita Naess. 1987. *Were They All Men? An Examination of Sex Roles in Prehistoric Society*. Stavanger, Norway: Arkeologist Museum I Stavanger.

Binford, Lewis R. 1962. "Archaeology as Anthropology." *American Antiquity* 28, no. 2: 217–25.

Binford, Lewis R. 1964. "A Consideration of Archaeological Research Design." *American Antiquity* 29, no. 4: 425–41.

Binford, Lewis R. 1965. "Archaeological Systematics and the Study of Culture Process." *American Antiquity* 31, no. 2: 203–10.

Binford, Lewis R. 1972. *An Archaeological Perspective*. New York: Seminar Press.

Binford, Lewis R. 1983. *In Pursuit of the Past: Decoding the Archaeological Record*. London: Thames and Hudson.

Boas, Frans. 1911. *Handbook of American Indian Languages*. Bureau of American Ethnology, Bulletin 40. Washington, DC: Government Print Office (Smithsonian Institution, Bureau of American Ethnology).

Boast, Robin, and Jim Enote. 2014. "Virtual Repatriation: It Is Neither Virtual nor Repatriation." In *Heritage in the Context of Globalization*, edited by Peter F. Biehl and Christopher Prescott, 103–13. New York: Springer.

Bourdieu, Pierre. 1977. *Outline of a Theory of Practice*. Cambridge: Cambridge University Press.

Bradfield, Wesley. 1929. *Cameron Creek Village: A Site in the Mimbres Area in Grant County, New Mexico*. Santa Fe, NM: School of American Research.

Brody, J. J. (1977) 2004. *Mimbres Painted Pottery*. Rev. ed. Santa Fe, NM: School for Advanced Research.

Brody, J. J. 1983. "Mimbres Painting." In *Mimbres Pottery: Ancient Art of the American Southwest*, edited by J. J. Brody, Catherine J. Scott, and Steven A. LeBlanc, 13–22. New York: Hudson Hills Press.

Brody, J. J., Catherine J. Scott, and Steven A. LeBlanc. 1983. *Mimbres Pottery: Ancient Art of the American Southwest*. New York: Hudson Hills Press.

Bryan, Bruce. 1927a. "The Galaz Ruin in the Mimbres Valley." *El Palacio* 23, no. 12: 323–37.

Bryan, Bruce. 1927b. "The Mimbres Expedition." *The Masterkey* 1, no. 4: 19–30.

Bryan, Bruce. 1931a. "Excavation of the Galaz Ruin." *The Masterkey* 4, no. 6: 179–89.

Bryan, Bruce. 1931b. "Excavation of the Galaz Ruin, Mimbres Valley, New Mexico." *Art and Archaeology* 32, no. 1: 35–42.

Bryan, Bruce. 1961. "Initial Report on Galaz Sherds." *The Masterkey* 35, no. 1: 13–18.

Cajete, Gregory. 2000. *Native Science: Natural Laws of Interdependence*. Santa Fe, NM: Clear Light Publishers.

Carr, Pat M. 1979. *Mimbres Mythology*. El Paso: University of Texas at El Paso.

Cheater, Angela P. 2003. *Social Anthropology: An Alternative Introduction*. Zimbabwe: Mambo Press.

Childe, Gordon V. 1929. *The Danube in Prehistory*. Oxford: Clarendon Press.

Claassen, Cheryl, and Rosemary Joyce. 1997. *Women in Prehistory: North America and Mesoamerica*. Philadelphia: University of Pennsylvania Press.

Colton, Harold S. 1939. *Prehistoric Culture Units and Their Relationships in Northern Arizona*. Museum of Northern Arizona Bulletin, No. 17. Flagstaff: Northern Arizona Society of Science and Art.

Colton, Harold S., and Lyndon Hargrave. 1937. *Handbook of Northern Arizona Pottery Wares*. Museum of Northern Arizona Bulletin, No. 11. New York: AMS Press.

Colwell-Chanthaphonh, Chip. 2010. *Living Histories: Native Americans and Southwestern Archaeology*. Lanham, MD: Rowman & Littlefield.

Colwell, Chip. 2020. "Collaboration Is Only a Tool to Decolonize the Museum." *Trajectoria* 1: 1–11.

Colwell, Chip, and T. J. Ferguson. 2014. "The Snow Capped Mountain and the Uranium Mine: Zuni Heritage and the Landscape-Scale in Cultural Resource Management." *Advances in Archaeological Practice* 2, no. 4: 234–54.

Conkey, Margaret, and Joan M. Gero. 1991. *Engendering Archaeology: Women and Prehistory*. Hoboken, NJ: Wiley-Blackwell.

Connell, Raewyn W. 1987. *Gender and Power: Society, the Person, and Sexual Politics*. Cambridge: Polity Press.

Cordell, Linda S., and Maxine E. McBrinn. 2016. *Archaeology of the Southwest*. 3rd ed. New York: Routledge.

Cosgrove, C. Burton, and Harriet S. Cosgrove. 1932. *The Swarts Ruin: A Typical Mimbres Site in Southwestern New Mexico*. Cambridge, MA: Harvard University, Papers of the Peabody Museum of American Archaeology and Ethnology 15, no. 1.

Creel, Darrell. 2006. *Excavations at the Old Town Ruin, Luna County, New Mexico, 1989–2003*. Santa Fe, NM: U.S. Bureau of Land Management, New Mexico State Office.

Cushing, Frank Hamilton. 1896. "Outlines of Zuni Creation Myths." In *13th Annual Report of the Bureau of Ethnology for the Years 1891–1892*, 321–447. Washington, DC: Government Printing Office.

Deloria, Vince, Jr. 2012. *The Metaphysics of Modern Existence*. Golden, CO: Fulcrum Publishing.

Dongoske, Kurt, T. J. Ferguson, and Leigh Jenkins. 1993. "Understanding the Past Through Hopi Oral History." *Native Peoples Magazine* 6, no. 2: 24–31.

Dozier, Edward. 1965. "Southwestern Social Units and Archaeology." *American Antiquity* 31, no. 1: 38–47.

Dozier, Edward. 1970. *The Pueblo Indians of North America.* Long Grove, IL: Waveland Press.

DuCros, Hillary, and Laurajane Smith. 1992. *Women in Archaeology: A Feminist Critique.* Canberra: Austrian National University.

Duff, Andrew I., T. J. Ferguson, Susan Bruning, and Peter Whiteley. 2008. "Collaborative Research in a Living Landscape: Pueblo Land, Culture, and History in West-Central New Mexico." *Archaeology Southwest* 22, no. 1: 1–24.

Duff, U. Francis. 1902. "The Ruins in the Mimbres Valley." *American Antiquarian* 24, no. 5: 397–400.

Duwe, Samuel, and Robert W. Preucel, eds. 2019. *The Continuous Path: Pueblo Movement and the Archaeology of Becoming.* Amerind Studies in Anthropology. Tucson: University of Arizona Press.

Eggan, Fred. 1950. *Social Organization of the Western Pueblo.* Chicago: University of Chicago Press.

Ehrenberg, Margaret R. 1989. *Women in Prehistory.* Norman: University of Oklahoma Press.

Ferguson, T. J. 1995. "An Anthropological Perspective on Zuni Land Use." In *Zuni and the Courts*, edited by Richard E. Hart, 103–20. Lawrence: University Press of Kansas.

Ferguson, T. J. 1996. "Native Americans and the Practice of Archaeology." *Annual Review of Anthropology* 25: 63–79.

Ferguson, T. J. 2003. *Yep Hisat Hoopoq'yagam Yeesiwa (Hopi Ancestors Were Once Here): Hopi-Hohokam Cultural Affiliation Study.* Kykotsmovi, AZ: Hopi Cultural Preservation Office.

Ferguson, T. J. 2004. "Academic, Legal, and Political Contexts of Social Identity and Cultural Affiliation Research in the Southwest." In *Identity, Feasting, and the Archaeology of the Greater Southwest*, edited by Barbara J. Mills, 27–41. Boulder: University Press of Colorado.

Ferguson, T. J., and Chip Colwell-Chanthaphonh. 2006. *History Is in the Land: Multivocal Tribal Traditions in Arizona's San Pedro Valley.* Tucson: University of Arizona.

Ferguson, T. J., Kurt E. Dongoske, Mike Yeatts, and Leigh H. Kuwanwisiwma. 2000. "Hopi Oral History and Archaeology." In *Working Together: Native Americans and Archaeologists*, edited by Kurt E. Dongoske, Mark Aldenderfer, and Karen Doehner, 45–60. Washington, DC: Society for American Archaeology.

Fewkes, J. Walter. 1914. "Archaeology of the Lower Mimbres Valley, New Mexico." *Smithsonian Miscellaneous Collections* 63, no. 10: 1–53.

Fewkes, J. Walter. 1915. "Prehistoric Remains in New Mexico. Explorations and Field-Work of the Smithsonian Institution in 1914." *Smithsonian Miscellaneous Collections* 65, no. 6: 62–72.

Fewkes, J. Walter. 1916. "Animal Figures in Prehistoric Pottery from Mimbres Valley, New Mexico." *American Anthropologist* 18, no. 4: 535–45.

Fewkes, J. Walter. 1923. "Designs on Prehistoric Pottery from the Mimbres Valley, New Mexico." *Smithsonian Miscellaneous Collections* 74, no. 6.

Fewkes, J. Walter. 1924. "Additional Designs on Prehistoric Mimbres Pottery, New Mexico." *Smithsonian Miscellaneous Collections* 76, no. 8.

Fuchs, Martin. 2009. "Bracketing [Belief], Or: The Locus and Status of 'Belief' in Cultural Analysis." *Journal of Social Anthropology and Cultural Studies* 6, no. 1: 1–23.

Gad, Christopher, Casper B. Jensen, and Brit R. Winthereik. 2015. "Practical Ontology: Worlds in STS and Anthropology." Osaka University Knowledge Archive (OUKA). https://ir.library.osaka-u.ac.jp.

Gadamer, Hans-Georg. 1991. *Plato's Dialectical Ethics: Phenomenological Interpretations Relating to the "Philebus,"* translated by R. M. Wallace. New Haven, CT: Yale University Press.

Gero, Joan M. 1991. "Genderlithics: Women's Roles in Stone Tool Production." In *Engendering Archaeology: Women and Prehistory*, edited by Joan M. Gero and Margaret W. Conkey, 163–93. Oxford: Blackwell.

Gero, Joan M., and Margaret W. Conkey. 1991. *Engendering Archaeology: Women and Prehistory.* Oxford: Blackwell.

Giddens, Anthony. 1984. *The Constitution of Society.* Berkeley: University of California Press.

Gilman, Patricia A., and Steven A. LeBlanc. 2017. *Mimbres Life and Society: The Mattocks Site of Southwestern New Mexico.* Tucson: University of Arizona Press.

Gilman, Patricia A., Marc Thompson, and Kristina C. Wyckoff. 2015. "Ritual Change and the Distant: Mesoamerican Iconography, Scarlet Macaws, and Great Kivas in the Mimbres Region of Southwestern New Mexico." *American Antiquity* 79: 90–107.

Gladwin, Winifred, and Harold S. Gladwin. 1934. *A Method for the Designation of Cultures and Their Variations.* Medallion Papers, No. 15. Globe, AZ: Gila Pueblo.

Govinda, Lama Anagarika. 1981. *The Inner Structure of the I Ching: The Book of Transformations.* New York: Wheelwright Press.

Graham, A. C. 1989. *Disputers of the Tao: Philosophical Argument in Ancient China.* Chicago: Open Court Publishing Company.

Gunderson, Lance H., and Crawford S. Holling. 2002. *Panarchy: Understanding Transformations in Human and Natural Systems.* Washington, DC: Island Press.

Habu, Junko, Clare Fawcett, and John M. Matsunaga. 2008. *Evaluating Multiple Narratives: Beyond Nationalist, Colonist, Imperialist Archaeologies.* New York: Springer.

Hall, David L., and Roger T. Ames. 1998. *Thinking from the Han Self, Truth, and Transcendence in Chinese and Western Culture.* Albany, NY: SUNY Press.

Harrington, John P. 1916. *Ethnography of the Tewa.* 29th Annual Report of the Bureau of American Ethnology. Washington, DC: Government Printing Office.

Haury, Emil W. 1936. *The Mogollon Culture of Southwestern New Mexico.* Globe, AZ: Medallion Gila Pueblo.

Hawkes, Christopher. 1954. "Archaeological Theory and Method: Some Suggestions from the Old World." *American Anthropologist* 56: 155–68.

Hegmon, Michelle. 2003. "Setting Theoretical Egos Aside: Issues and Theory in North American Archaeology." *American Antiquity* 68, no. 2: 213–43.

Hegmon, Michelle. 2008. "Structure and Agency in Southwest Archaeology." In *The Social Construction of Communities: Agency, Structure, and Identity in the Prehispanic Southwest*, 217–32. Lanham, MD: Rowman & Littlefield.

Hegmon, Michelle, and Stephanie Kulow. 2005. "Painting as Agency, Style as Structure: Analyses of Mimbres Pottery Designs from Southwest New Mexico." *Journal of Archaeological Method and Theory* 12: 313–34.

Hegmon, Michelle, James R. McGrath, F. Michael O'Hara III, and Will G. Russell. 2018. "Mimbres Pottery Designs in their Social Context." In *New Perspectives on Mimbres Archaeology: Three Millennia of Human Occupation in the Desert Southwest*, edited by Patricia A. Gilman, Roger Anyon, and Barbara Roth, 149–68. Tucson: University of Arizona Press.

Hegmon, Michelle, Scott G. Ortman, and Jeannett L. Mobley-Tanaka. 2000. "Women, Men, and the Organization of Space." In *Women & Men in the Prehistoric Southwest: Labor, Power, & Prestige*, edited by Patricia L. Crown. Santa Fe, NM: School of American Research Advanced Seminar Series.

Hegmon, Michelle, and Wenda R. Trevathan. 1996. "Gender, Anatomical Knowledge, and Pottery Production: Implications of an Anatomically Unusual Birth Depicted on Mimbres Pottery from Southwestern New Mexico." *American Antiquity* 61, no. 4: 747–54.

Henshaw, Henry W. 1879. "Cliff-House and Cave on Diamond Creek, New Mexico." In *Report Upon United States Geographical Surveys West of the One Hundredth Meridian Volume 7. Reports Upon Archaeological and Ethnological Collections from Vicinity of Santa Barbara, California Interior Tribes*, edited by Frederick W. Putnam, 370–71. Washington, DC: Government Printing Office.

Hewett, Edgar Lee. 1906. *Antiquities of the Jemez Plateau, New Mexico*. Bureau of American Ethnology Bulletin No. 32. Washington, DC: Government Printing Office.

Hodder, Ian. 1991. "The Current Theoretical Debate." In *Processual and Postprocessual Archaeologies*, edited by Robert Preucel. Carbondale: Center for Archaeological Investigations, University of Illinois.

Hodder, Ian. 1994. "The Interpretation of Documents and Material Culture." In *Handbook of Qualitative Research*, edited by N. K. Denzin and Y. S. Lincoln, 393–402. Thousand Oaks, CA: Sage Publications.

Hodder, Ian. 1999. *The Archaeological Process*. Oxford: Blackwell.

Hodder, Ian. 2004. *Archaeology Beyond Dialogue*. Salt Lake City: University of Utah Press.

Hodder, Ian. 2008. "Multivocality and Social Archaeology." In *Evaluating Multiple Narratives: Beyond Nationalist, Colonialist, and Imperialist Archaeologies*, edited by Junko Habu, Clare Fawcett, and John Matsunaga, 196–200. New York: Springer Press.

Hodder, Ian, and Scott Hutson. 2003. *Reading the Past: Current Approaches to Interpretation in Archaeology*. Cambridge: Cambridge University Press.

Ito, Atsunori. 2016. *Re-Collection and Sharing Traditional Knowledge, Memories, Information, and Images: Challenges and the Prospects on Creating Collaborative Catalog*. Senri Ethnological Reports 137. Osaka: National Museum of Ethnology.

Ito, Atsunori. 2017. *Collections Review on the Katsina Dolls Labeled "Hopi" in the National Museum of Ethnology: Reconnecting Source Communities with Museum Collections 1*. Senri Ethnological Reports 140. Osaka: National Museum of Ethnology.

Ito, Atsunori. 2019. *Collections Review on 24 Items Labeled "Hopi" in the Tenri University Sankokan Museum: Reconnecting Source Communities with Museum Collections 2*. Info-Forum Museum Resources 2. Osaka: National Museum of Ethnology.

Ito, Atsunori. 2020. *Collections Review on 186 Items Labeled "Hopi" in the National Museum of Ethnology: Reconnecting Source Communities with Museum Collections 3*. Info-Forum Museum Resources 3. Osaka: National Museum of Ethnology.

Ito, Atsunori, Kathy Dougherty, and Kelley Hays-Gilpin. 2020. *Collections Review on 446 Silverworks and Related Items Labeled "Hopi" in the Museum of Northern Arizona: Reconnecting Source Communities with Museum Collections 4*. Info-Forum Museum Resources 4. Osaka: National Museum of Ethnology.

Ito, Atsunori, Candice Lomahaftewa, and Chip Colwell. 2021. *Collections Review on 38 Silverworks Labeled "Hopi" in the Denver Museum of Nature & Science: Reconnecting Source Communities with Museum Collections 5*. Info-Forum Museum Resources 5. Osaka: National Museum of Ethnology.

Jenks, Albert E. 1930a. "In the Field: University of Minnesota." *El Palacio* 29, no. 4–1: 150–51.

Jenks, Albert E. 1930b. "Pottery of Mimbreños and Gila." *Bulletin of the Minneapolis Institute of Arts* 19, no. 33: 162–65.

Jenks, Albert E. 1931. "The Significance of Mended Bowls in Mimbres Culture." *El Palacio* 31, no. 10–11: 151–72.

Jenks, Albert E. 1932a. "Architectural Plans of Geometric Art on Mimbres Bowls." *El Palacio* 33, no. 3–6: 21–64.

Jenks, Albert E. 1932b. "Geometric Designs on Mimbres Bowls." *Art and Archaeology* 33, no. 3: 137, 139, 158.

Jiang, Xinyan. 2013. *Chinese Dialectical Thinking—the Yin Yang Model*. Wiley Online Library.

Johnson, Matthew. 1999. *Archaeological Theory: An Introduction*. Malden, MA: Blackwell Publishers.

Kabotie, Fred. 1982. *Designs from the Ancient Mimbreños with Hopi Interpretation*. Salisbury, CT: Lime Rock Press.

Keesing, Roger M. 1974. "Theories of Culture." *Annual Review of Anthropology* 3: 73–97.

Kidder, Alfred V. 1924. *Southwestern Archaeology, Excavations at Pecos*. New Haven, CT: Department of Archaeology, Yale University.

Kidder, Alfred V. 1927. "Southwestern Archaeological Conference." *Palacio* 23: 554–61.

Kluckhole, Clyde. (1940) 1972. "The Conceptual Structure in Middle American Studies." In *Contemporary Archaeology*, edited by Mark Leone, 78–84. Carbondale: Southern Illinois University Press.

Kroeber, Alfred. 1916. "Zuni Potsherds." New York: Anthropological Papers of the American Museum of Natural History 18, no. 1.

Kuwanwisiwma, Leigh J., and T. J. Ferguson. 2004. "Ang Kuktota: Hopi Ancestral Sites and Cultural Landscapes." *Expedition* 46, no. 2: 25–29.

LeBlanc, Steve A. 1983. *The Mimbres People: Ancient Pueblo Painters of the American Southwest*. London: Thames and Hudson.

LeBlanc, Steve A. 2004. *Painted by a Distant Hand: Mimbres Pottery from the American Southwest*. Cambridge, MA: Peabody Museum.

LeBlanc, Steve A., and M. M. Ellis. 2001. "The Individual Artist in Mimbres Culture: Painted Bowl Production and Specialization." Poster presented at the 66th annual meeting of the Society for American Archaeology, New Orleans.

LeBlanc, Steve A., and Michael E. Whalen. 1980. *An Archaeological Synthesis of South-central and Southwestern New Mexico*. Albuquerque: Office of Contract Archaeology, University of New Mexico.

Maciocia, Giovanni. 1989. *The Foundations of Chinese Medicine.* London: Churchill Livingstone, an imprint of Elsevier.

Marshall, Yvonne. 1998. "Intimate Relations Issue." *World Archaeology* 29, no. 3: 311–16.

McKern, William C. 1939. "The Midwestern Taxonomic Method as an Aid to Archaeological Culture Study." *American Antiquity* 4, no. 4: 301–13.

Mills, Barbara J., and T. J. Ferguson. 1998. "Preservation and Research of Sacred Sites by the Zuni Indian Tribe of New Mexico." *Human Organization* 57, no. 1: 30–42.

Ming-Dao, Deng. 1990. *Scholar Warrior: An Introduction to the Tao in Everyday Life*. New York: HarperCollins Publishers.

Moore, Jerry. 2009. *Visions of Culture: An Annotated Reader*. Lanham, MD: Rowman & Littlefield.

Moore, Jenny, and Eleanor Scott. 1997. *Invisible People and Processes: Writing Gender and Childhood into European Archaeology*. London: Leicester University Press.

Moulard, Barbara L., and John B. Taylor. 1984. *Within the Underworld Sky: Mimbres Ceramics Art in Context*. Santa Fe, NM: Twelvetrees Press.

Moss, Madonna L. 2005. "Rifts in the Theoretical Landscape of Archaeology in the United States: A Comment on Hegmon and Watkins." *American Antiquity* 70, no. 3: 581–87.

Motokawa, Tatsuo. 1989. "Sushi Science and Hamburger Science." *Perspectives in Biology and Medicine* 32, no. 4: 489–504.

Naranjo, Tessie. 1995. "Thoughts on Migration by Santa Clara Pueblo." *Journal of Anthropological Archaeology* 14: 247–50.

Naranjo, Tessie. 2008. "Life as Movement: A Tewa View of Community and Identity." In *The Social Construction of Communities: Agency, Structure, and Identity in the Prehispanic Southwest*, edited by Mark D. Varien and James M. Potter, 251–62. Walnut Creek, CA: AltaMira Press.

Needham, Joseph. 1956. *Science and Civilisation in China*. Vol. 2 of *History of Scientific Thought*. Cambridge: Cambridge University Press.

Nelson, Margaret C. 1999. *Mimbres During the Twelfth Century: Abandonment, Continuity, and Reorganization*. Tucson: University of Arizona Press.

Nelson, Margaret C., and Michelle Hegmon. 2010. *Mimbres Lives and Landscapes*. A School for Advanced Research Popular Southwestern Archaeology Book. Santa Fe, NM: School of Advanced Research Press.

Nesbitt, Paul H. 1931. *The Ancient Mimbreños, Based on Investigations at the Mattocks Ruin, Mimbres Valley, New Mexico*. Beloit, WI: Logan Museum Bulletin Number 4.

Ortiz, Alfonso. 1969. *The Tewa World: Space, Time, Being and Becoming in a Pueblo Soci*ety. Chicago: University of Chicago Press.

Parsons, Elsie Clews. 1925. *The Pueblo of Jemez*. New Haven, CT: Papers of the Phillips Academy Southwestern Expedition, No. 3.

Parsons, Elsie Clews. 1929. *The Social Organization of the Tewa of New Mexico*. Menasha, WI: Memoirs of the American Anthropological Association, No. 36.

Peat, David. 2002. *Blackfoot Physics: A Journey into the Native American Universe*. Newburyport, MA: Weiser Books.

Potter, James M. 2000. "Pots, Parties, and Politics: Communal Feasting in the American Southwest." *American Antiquity* 65, no. 3: 471–82.

Preucel, Robert W. 1991. *Processual and Postprocessual Archaeologies: Multiple Ways of Knowing the Past*. Carbondale: Center for Archaeological Investigations, Southern Illinois University.

Redman, Charles. 2005. "Resilience Theory and Archaeology." *American Anthropologist* 107, no. 1: 70–77.

Roth, Barbara J., Patricia A. Gilman, and Roger Anyon. 2018. *New Perspectives on Mimbres Archaeology: Three Millennia of Human Occupation in the North American Southwest*. Tucson: University of Arizona Press.

Salmon, Merrilee. 1992. *Philosophical Models for Postprocessual Archaeology*. Boston Studies in the Philosophy of Science book series. New York: Springer.

Sandor, Jonathan A. 1992. "Long-term Effects of Prehistoric Agriculture on Soils: Examples from New Mexico and Peru." In *Soils in Archaeology: Landscape Evolution and Human Occupation*, edited by Vance T. Holliday, 217–45. Washington, DC: Smithsonian Institution Press.

Sandor, Jonathan A., Paul L. Gersper, and John W. Hawley. 1990. "Prehistoric Agricultural Terraces and Soils in the Mimbres Area, New Mexico." *World Archaeology* 22: 70–86.

Sassaman, Kenneth E. 1992. "Lithic Technology and the Hunter-Gatherer Sexual Division of Labor." *North American Archaeologist* 13: 249–62.

Schaafsma, Polly. 1999. "Tlalocs, Kachinas, Sacred Bundles, and Related Symbolism in the Southwest." In *The Casas Grandes World*, edited by Curtis F. Schaafsma and Carroll L. Riley, 164–92. Salt Lake City: University of Utah Press.

Schachner, Gregory. 2001. "Ritual Control and Transformation in Middle-Range Societies: An Example from the American Southwest." *Journal of Anthropological Archaeology* 20: 168–94.

Schneider, Arnd. 2011. "Unfinished Dialogues: Notes toward an Alternative History of Art and Anthropology." In *Made to Be Seen: Perspectives on the History of Visual Anthropology*, edited by Marcus Banks and Jay Ruby. Oslo: Universitetet I Oslo.

Scott, Jorden. 2020. "Connections between the Mimbreños People and Local Avian Species." Master's thesis, Department of Anthropology, New Mexico State University, Las Cruces, New Mexico.

Shafer, Harry J. 1995. "Architecture and Symbolism in Transitional Pueblo Development in the Mimbres Valley, SW New Mexico." *Journal of Field Archaeology* 22, no. 1: 23–47.

Shafer, Harry J. 2003. *Mimbres Archaeology at the NAN Ranch Ruin*. 1st ed. Albuquerque: University of New Mexico Press.

Skibo, James, and Michael Schiffer. 2009. *People and Things: A Behavioral Approach to Material Culture*. New York: Springer.

Steward, Julian H. 1937. "Ecological Aspects of Southwestern Society." *Anthropos* 32: 87–104.

Steward, Julian H. 1942. "The Direct Historical Approach to Archaeology." *American Antiquity* 7, no. 4: 337–43.

Steward, Julian H., and Frank M. Setzler. 1938. "Function and Configuration in Archaeology." *American Antiquity* 4, no. 1: 4–10.

Swentzell, Rina. 1991. "Levels of Truth: Southwest Archaeologists and Anasazi/ Pueblo People." In *Puebloan Past and Present: Papers in Honor of Stewart Peckham*, edited by Meliha S. Duran and David T. Kirkpatrick, 177–81. Albuquerque: Archaeological Society of New Mexico.

Swentzell, Rina. 1993. "Mountain Form, Village Form: Unity in the Pueblo World." In *Ancient Land, Ancestral Places: Paul Logsdon in the Pueblo Southwest*, edited by Stephen H. Lekson, 139–47. Santa Fe: Museum of New Mexico Press.

Swidler, N., Kurt Dongoske, Roger Anyon, and A. S. Downer. 1997. *Native Americans and Archaeologists: Stepping Stones to Common Ground*. Walnut Creek, CA: AltaMira Press.

Taylor, Walter W. (1948) 1983. *A Study of Archaeology*. 1983 edition, with a forward by Patty Jo Watson. Carbondale: Center for Archaeological Investigations, Southern Illinois University.

Taylor, William. 1898. "The Pueblos and Ancient Mines near Allison, New Mexico." *American Antiquarian* 20, no. 5: 258–61.

Thompson, Mac. 1994. "The Evolution and Dissemination of Mimbres Iconography." In *Kachinas in the Pueblo World*, edited by Polly Schaafsma, 93–105. Albuquerque: University of New Mexico Press.

Thompson, Mac. 1999. "Knife-wing: A Prominent Mesoamerican, Mimbres, and Pueblo Icon." In *Sixty Years of Mogollon Archaeology: Papers from the Ninth Mogollon Conference, Silver City, New Mexico, 1996*, edited by Stephanie M. Whittlesey, 145–50. Tucson: SRI Press.

Tilley, Christopher. 2014. *Material Culture and Text: The Art of Ambiguity*. New York: Routledge Library Editions: Archaeology.

Titiev, Mischa. (1944) 1992. *Old Oraibi: A Study of the Hopi Indians of Third Mesa*. Albuquerque: University of New Mexico Press.

Trigger, Bruce. 1989. *A History of Archaeological Thought*. Cambridge: Cambridge University Press.

Trigger, Bruce. 2006. *A History of Archaeological Thought*. 2nd ed. Cambridge: Cambridge University Press.

Trigger, Bruce. 2008. "'Alternative Archaeologies' in Historical Perspective." In *Evaluating Multiple Narratives: Beyond Nationalist, Colonialist, and Imperialist Archaeologies*, edited by Junko Habu, Clare Fawcett, and John Matsunaga, 187–95. New York: Springer Press.

Varien, Mark D., and James M. Potter. 2008. *The Social Construction of Communities: Agency, Structure, and Identity in the Prehispanic Southwest*. Lanham, MD: Rowman & Littlefield.

Walde, Dale, and Noreen D. Willows. 1991. *The Archaeology of Gender*. Alberta: Archaeological Association of the University of Calgary.

Watkins, Joe. 2001. *Indigenous Archaeology: American Indian Values and Scientific Practice*. Walnut Creek, CA: AltaMira Press.

Watkins, Joe. 2003. "Beyond the Margin: American Indians, First Nations, and Archaeology in North America." *American Antiquity* 68: 273–85.

Watson, Patty Jo, Steven A. LeBlanc, and Charles L. Redman. 1971. *Explanation in Archaeology: An Explicitly Scientific Approach*. New York: Columbia University Press.

Watson, Patty Jo, Steven A. LeBlanc, and Charles L. Redman. 1984. *Archaeological Explanation: The Scientific Method in Archeology*. New York: Columbia University Press.

Webster, Clement L. 1891. "Preliminary Notes on the Archaeology of Southwestern New Mexico." *The American Naturalist* 25: 767–70.

Webster, Clement L. 1912a. "Some Burial Customs Practiced by the Ancient People of the Southwest." *The Archaeological Bulletin* 3, no. 3: 69–79.

Webster, Clement L. 1912b. "Archaeological and Ethnological Researches in Southwestern New Mexico, Part I." *The Archaeological Bulletin* 3, no. 4: 101–15.

Webster, Clement L. 1913a. "Archaeological and Ethnological Researches in Southwestern New Mexico, Part II." *The Archaeological Bulletin* 4, no. 1: 14–20.

Webster, Clement L. 1913b. "Archaeological and Ethnological Researches in Southwestern New Mexico, Part III." *The Archaeological Bulletin* 4, no. 2: 43–48.

Webster, Clement L. 1914a. "Archaeological and Ethnological Researches in Southwestern New Mexico, Part IV." *The Archaeological Bulletin* 5, no. 2: 19–26.

Webster, Clement L. 1914b. "Archaeological and Ethnological Researches in Southwestern New Mexico, Part V." *The Archaeological Bulletin* 5, no. 3: 44–46.

White, Leslie A. 1959. "The Concept of Culture." *American Anthropologist* 61, no. 2: 227–51.

Wilhelm, Richard, Cary Fink Baynes, and C. G Jung. 1950. *The I Ching, or Book of Changes: The Richard Wilhelm Translation*. Bollingen Series, 19. New York: Pantheon Books.

Willey, Gordon R., and Philip Phillips. 1958. "Part I. An Operational Basis for Culture-Historical Integration." In *Method and Theory in American Archaeology*, 9–57. Chicago: University of Chicago Press.

Willey, Gordon R., and Jeremy Sabloff. (1974) 1993. *A History of American Archaeology*. 3rd ed. New York: W. H. Freeman and Company.

Zhang, Dongsun. 1946. *Zhishi Yu Wenhua* [Knowledge and Culture]. Shanghai: Shangwu Yinshu Guan.

Index

About the Author

Fumi Arakawa is the director of the University Museum and a professor in the Department of Anthropology at New Mexico State University. He is also a research associate at the Crow Canyon Archaeological Center.

ABOUT THE CONTRIBUTORS

Octavius Seowtewa is the head medicine man for the Newekwe/Galazy medicine society and also a member of the Eagle Down medicine society. He is a supervisor for the Zuni Cultural Resources Advisory Team (ZCRAT). Octavius has been involved with numerous museum projects not only in the United States but also in Japan and in the Netherlands. He has reviewed an innumerable amount of Zuni cultural remains at museums for over twenty years.

Jim Enote is a Zuni tribal member and CEO of the Colorado Plateau Foundation. His services for the past forty years include work with natural resources, cultural heritage resources, philanthropy, and arts assignments for many organizations, such as UNESCO, International Secretariat for Water, National Geographic Society, US Bureau of Indian Affairs, US National Park Service, Zuni Tribe, and several major charitable foundations, museums, and universities.